KENNETH TURNER'S
FLOWER STYLE

THE ART OF
FLORAL DESIGN
AND DECORATION

PHOTOGRAPHS BY
John Miller and Fritz von der Schulenburg

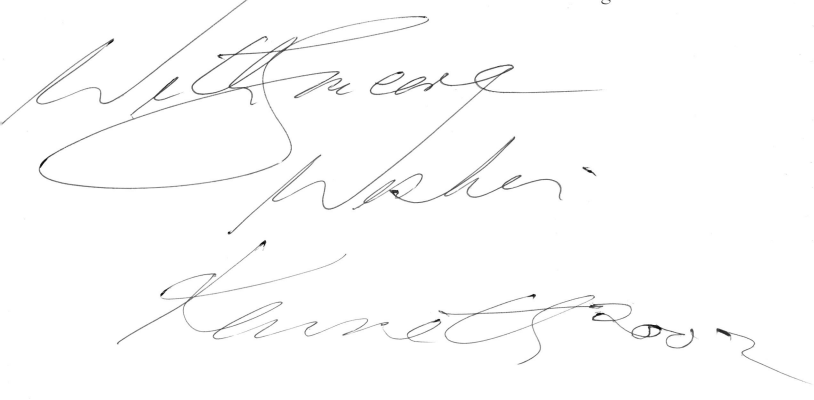

PHOENIX ILLUSTRATED

Copyright © 1989, 1994 George Weidenfeld & Nicolson Ltd

First published in 1989 by George Weidenfeld & Nicolson Ltd

Reprinted in 1994

This paperback edition first published in 1997 by Phoenix Illustrated
Orion Publishing Group, Orion House
5, Upper St. Martin's Lane
London WC2H 9EA

British Library Cataloguing-in-Publication Data
A catalogue record for this book is available from
the British Library

ISBN 1-85799-932-0

Designed by Harry Green
Phototypeset by Keyspools, Golborne, Lancashire
Colour separations by Newsele Litho Ltd
Printed in Italy by Printers Srl, Trento
Bound by L.E.G.O., Vicenza

Captions for previous pages and prelims are on page 160

FOR MY MOTHER

WHO GAVE ME SO MUCH

AND ASKED FOR SO LITTLE

AND WHO SHARED

IN MY LOVE OF NATURE

CONTENTS

ORIGINS AND IDEAS

The aim in decorating should always be to exceed expectation; to surprise and amaze the beholder; to stimulate the eye and the mind; to celebrate the inherent beauty of the natural world.

My own path to where I am now (I am considered London's foremost floral decorator) did not at the time seem a particularly direct one. As a child I was fascinated by nature and wild flowers and would buy packets of seeds rather than sweets with my pocket money. My parents and particularly my grandfather fostered this interest, encouraging me to learn more about it and teaching me all they knew, but I had no clear ambition to be a florist (there were no floral decorators in those days); I just knew I was born to do something associated with flowers and gardening.

I foolishly left school as early as I possibly could and went to work on a private estate under an old gardener who would buy vegetables and pass them off as home-grown when the kitchen-garden ran out; he was bone idle, but as a result I learnt a lot and the family were very kind to me. From there I joined a local nursery. On seeing how much I already knew, the owner, Mr Epstein, persuaded me and my parents that I would get nowhere in the gardening world unless I went to college and studied horticulture to give some formal training and scientific background to my hands-on experience. Much to my amazement, I sailed through the entrance exams and got a scholarship to Greenmount Horticultural College and then went on to Reading University where I took the course in ornamental horticulture. This taught me about the laying out of gardens, the principles of design and the importance of planning and gave me a wonderful grounding in the way shrubs grow, what blooms when and how to maintain continuity of flowering and colour in a garden all the year round. However, it also showed me that a career in horticulture was not for me and a lecturer advised me that if I wanted to work with flowers as a decorator I should go and learn the fundamentals of a flower shop. So I got a job in Oxford, working first for a flower-seller in the market, then moving on to David Crutchley's where the team working there were marvellous to me.

After a while they suggested that I move to live and work in London. It was my first real step in the right direction. Unfortunately, I was most unhappy in my first job. I had to scrub clean the pots and containers that were sent up from the country covered with moss and lichen; I hated doing it as it was completely alien to my love of all things wild and natural. One day, a lady – I never knew her name nor had a chance to thank her – took pity on me and told me that I ought to be with Pulbrook and Gould. She promptly telephoned them and they offered me a job. Lady Pulbrook and Miss Gould were the most innovative florists of the day, society florists based in Knightsbridge. I learnt a tremendous amount whilst I was there and they gave me an entrée to a world whose doors would otherwise have remained closed. Today that world lies at the heart of my livelihood and I am eternally grateful for the introduction and opportunities they gave me. I stayed ten years, rising to become head decorator, and it was during that time that my ideas were first really nurtured and I was encouraged to develop them. My first great success was with planted platters – large open plates which I filled with moss, stones and odd bits of wood and bark to create a wild and desolate landscape or gentle

At home with my two dogs Wags and Bumble, who go everywhere with me, much to the surprise of some of my clients.

woodland scene. They were in constant demand and I eventually realized that I would be freer to pursue my more unusual ideas if I set up on my own.

I left and, refusing all offers of backing, I was determined to prove myself and succeed in my own right. My junior from Pulbrooks, Jacqueline Horne, one of the most enthusiastic people I know, joined me and together we worked out of my flat in Marylebone, where there were flowers all over the place, even in the bath. It was hell for my flat-mate, who suffered from hayfever, until Jacqui found the basement premises in Avery Row in the heart of Mayfair. It was like a rat warren when we arrived and we transformed it, finding the front door and the furniture in a skip. After a few years we took over the rest of the house; meanwhile the business grew and grew until lack of space brought us round the corner to our present address, Brook Manor in Brook Street.

Floral decoration has developed out of all recognition since I first worked in

My team and I decorating the shop front of our former premises in Avery Row with an elaborate frame of privet.

the business in the 1960s. It wasn't even accepted as a concept in those days, and although even today the vast majority of flower arrangers and florists remain untouched by the extraordinary advances I, and a handful of others, have made in this field, a small percentage have modified their ideas and an even tinier one revolutionized their way of thinking. Few, however, show any spark of originality in their creations.

Thirty years ago flower arranging was almost the sole preserve of women; male florists were a rarity and looked on askance. Now, of course, there are many. One of the main differences in the practice of floristry between then and now was the formality of the art at that time. Even where the displays themselves employed the loose country look first introduced by Constance Spry, they tended to be limited and constrained – flowers were only acceptable in certain prescribed places and were never used as freely as they are now. Every single stem – every daffodil, every tulip – had to be wired so it could be adapted to its allotted space (rather than choosing a flower to fit), but fortunately that time is over now and only a very old-fashioned florist would insist on it. Everything had to be pristine, spruce and formal, and there was no place for the more rustic materials like birch and moss. Now the value of moss is almost universally recognized and it is used liberally as a means of softening the visual impact of displays, rather as a skirting is used to disguise the join between floor and wall. Special suppliers cultivate and gather it and it is bought in quality by florists wanting to create a natural look.

A typical job for a client in those days would consist of a pedestal here, a pedestal there and perhaps a few set-piece table decorations. We still do these, but they are of a different kind – the pedestal is no longer a device for mounting a display but an integral part of the decoration, consisting perhaps of branches of birch or an antique statue or urn. I like to include a mixture of types of decoration and flowers – so-called pedestals, huge groups with trees, garlands – a variety of decorations which loosely conform to a theme. The whole concept of decorating has changed; clients have gradually come to ask more and more as they realized how much a floral decorator could do for them. Now I create themes and ideas which are at the heart of an occasion rather than ornaments peripheral to it and which may include the china and linen for the table settings, hangings and a complete transformation of a room, rooms or even an entire building.

Even the conduct of business today is in stark contrast with the informality of the days when I would accompany Lady Pulbrook on a visit to a client; we would talk about aspects of the job – location and so on – and would be commissioned without a mention of cost, let alone preparing an itemized estimate, as is customary now. These days the props we use –even if we hire them – never mind the flowers, can be so expensive that it is almost impossible to tailor requirements without some idea of the budget.

My move away from formality and traditional props like the wrought-iron pedestal was an instinctive reaction against attempts to dominate nature that never really worked. I hate forced flowers – sometimes you see stems or branches contorted by the florist's attempt to make them go the way they want, but it's counter-productive. You should select with care, look at the stem you choose for a particular place and see if it's the right shaped branch for that spot; if it's not, choose another, and use the original stem elsewhere, so that when you've finished the display looks as natural as possible.

A knowledge of the mechanics of floristry as well as imagination is fundamental to the creation of a successful decoration. Methods of anchoring flowers and foliage, the question of balance, how to lengthen stems, the choice of container, presentation are all basics that every florist acquires and every amateur flower arranger should know something about even if the art is not mastered completely. My understanding of the growth pattern and the flowering habits of trees, shrubs and flowers, learnt at Reading, has been enormously important in contributing to my success as a floral decorator. Obviously it is not practical for everyone with an interest in flowers, gardening and decorating to study these things in detail, but you should at least remain constantly aware of the hidden implications of a decorative scheme, whether it is for use in the garden itself as a planting plan or inside as a feature or display. At the simplest and most practical level foreknowledge may suggest avoiding the use of a certain flower within an arrangement designed to last a week if you know that it usually drops and turns brown at the edges after twenty-four hours, whereas if the decoration were for a single dinner party it wouldn't matter.

It is terribly important not to see a decoration in isolation from its surroundings: it is part of a whole. You would not use a cup and saucer that didn't match: no more should you set a display on a tablecloth or against a background entirely alien to it. Decorations and their environs should be complementary, not dissonant, and if you are making a decoration for a particular spot it is essential to tailor shape, colour and feel to the overall effect that will be created. Ultimately I'm seeking a natural look. Nature does not jar the eye yet is full of surprises. If you take nature as a model and emulate her you cannot go far wrong.

The vital thing about any decoration is movement: movement and surprise. If a decoration looks static it is a failure. A large decoration should be branchy or loose with lots of foliage creating the basic shape and then filled in from there. But on no account should the shape be precisely symmetrical, and the outline should be broken up, perhaps by a trailing branch or a splash of colour or both. It doesn't matter what materials you use as long as you have an eye to the overall balance. You must consciously think: I need height, I need some branches to sweep down there, I need ivy or something similar to soften the line. If you do not think through what you are trying to achieve the result will be a shambles.

Decorations for large parties can take from a few hours to several days to put together. We usually make up the smaller decorations in the workroom but all the rest of the raw materials are delivered direct to the venue. Here we are just beginning to set up a reception at Brixton Academy.

Colour is another essential ingredient and requires careful consideration even if in the end the result is fairly monochrome, using whites with a touch of green for instance, which can look magnificent. Personally I quite like clashing colours – corals, reds, anything rich – although they have to be used with care. A russet orange and deep red might look superb combined in a decoration, but substitute a yellow for the orange and the same piece could be rendered unacceptable.

Season is also central to the choice of materials. It goes against the grain to pretend spring has arrived in November or December and it deeply offends my sense of the natural order of things. Each flower should only be used in its proper season. During a November visit to New York I went to see one of my clients (who has a truly magnificent apartment) to advise her on decorations for the Thanksgiving holiday. In the middle of the most fabulous dining room she had set two silver containers full of white tulips. They were beautiful, but they were utterly wrong, for the occasion and for the time of year, so I told her to get rid of them and never to let me see her using white tulips at that time of year again. If they had been white roses the crime would not have been so great because some roses are still in flower in November (in fact they are among the few plants it is acceptable to use the whole year round), but tulips belong to the New Year and to spring.

It should go without saying that a decoration will only ever look as good as the

I have used the same suppliers at Covent Garden Market for years and the excellent service they provide has been invaluable to me. The new premises at Nine Elms in South London lacks romance, but is none the less very functional.

materials used in it, though some florists seem to overlook this simple fact: limp stems or jaded blooms will never help a decoration and all too frequently make a grand design look ill-conceived. Healthy, fresh flowers and foliage, on the other hand, allow even the simplest arrangement to be memorable. As few gardens are large enough to supply all needs, it is worth building up a relationship with a local flower seller or florist. Not only will you then be treated as a preferred customer, you are also highly likely to benefit from the odd 'bargain' price and discount for special occasions. I buy nearly all the flowers and plants for the shop and our work direct from Covent Garden Market, where certain suppliers have looked after me for years and who will always look out for something special for me. I still go myself whenever I can as there's no substitute for choosing the raw materials oneself.

A career in the flower business is certainly no easy option and there are no

short cuts: it has taken me twenty years to build up the business as it is now. The working day is extremely long – the market opens at three o'clock in the morning – and it is sometimes necessary to work all hours to get a job finished in time. If a client has ordered a dozen table decorations for a party there's no leeway in the timing. If they don't arrive in time not only will you not be used again by that client but his or her network of contacts will know all about it too (although of course there is a flip side to this coin, if the decorations are a success). The joy of the flower business is that new challenges constantly present themselves and a new idea can open up endless opportunities and possibilities – like, for instance, my development of the use of dried flowers, which has revolutionized the industry, and, later, the innovation of the use of wild flowers, herbs and vegetables alongside 'conventional' flowers, now completely accepted and widely adopted by other decorators.

Each job represents a challenge and an opportunity to do something brilliant and new, but there are areas that I am already aware are ripe for development and a fresh approach. There is more to be done with still lifes, landscape scenes and tableaus. I used to paint when I was younger and I would like to return to this one

LEFT I get shells, pebbles, driftwood, fungi and other rustic materials from John Spikes, who spends his days combing the seashore and woodlands of South Wales, making deliveries to London as infrequently as possible.

Dried flowers are supplied to me by specialist growers and agencies. This farm in Malvern, Worcestershire is one of the least commercial and most charming.

Sitting in the shop with a range of dried flower decorations, which we sell side by side with those of fresh flowers and my range of scented candles, pot pourri and body-care products.

day to explore more fully the relationship between the two arts. The one thing I long to be asked to create is a floral ballet. Stage design has always interested me but this would be taking it one step further, dressing the ballerinas in flowers as well as creating a floral tableau for the set: imagine, for instance, the ballerinas as nymphs dancing through real waterfalls in *Swan Lake*. Roy Strong once commissioned me to use my creative powers for the opening night of an exhibition, 'The Mask of Beauty', at the National Portrait Gallery. This entailed recreating the landscape settings of the portraits, making the pictures come alive. The whole gallery was transformed, right down to the floor which was ankle deep in autumn leaves. The guests went home filthy and sneezing but the evening was a tremendous success. I found the experience of working in the round tremendously stimulating and I hope I will get the chance to develop some ideas based on this concept more fully.

Ideas and opportunities feed off each other, and I hope in this book to show that by following certain broad principles and with a little imagination anyone with an interest in flowers and decorating can create a decoration or decorative scheme to be proud of.

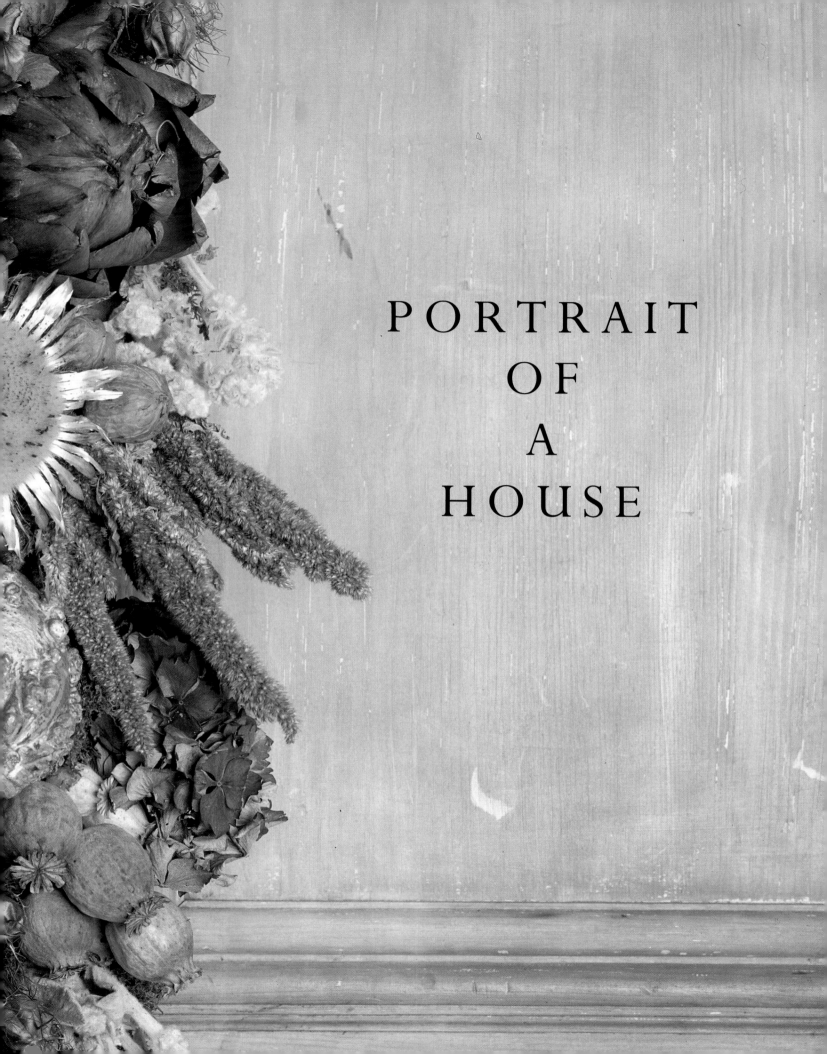

PORTRAIT
OF
A
HOUSE

THE GERM OF AN IDEA

The home should be a reflection of its owner's personality, an extension of the self, somewhere to escape to, somewhere to enjoy and somewhere to love. Before starting work on your home, you should think about what you want it to be, what roles it will have to play, how you can tailor what already exists and consciously set about fulfilling that vision. Never be afraid to overturn a received wisdom in design or decoration: do what seems right to you, if you don't like it you can change it.

Although an Irishman, I believe very strongly that an Englishman's home should be his castle and treasure the privacy that my own four walls give. I first came to this house (in Wandsworth, south London) in 1983. Before that I lived north of the Thames in a small house in Fulham with a tiny garden which, with my mania for collecting, I soon found myself growing out of. I desperately wanted to find a cottage in the country that I could escape to at weekends away from the hurly-burly of London and the business. The country and the sea have an eternal attraction for me, no doubt because that was the environment in which I grew up and which holds so many childhood memories for me.

I trudged to and fro the Sussex area for over two years looking in vain for my dream home until one day I realized that once south of the river and over the hill from Wandsworth Bridge I was almost in the countryside anyway. There were open spaces, tall leafy trees, bird-song, the thrilling prospect of a large garden and a quasi-rural existence that could be a fair approximation of the real thing. I immediately began to trawl the area, found this road and saw this house. I fell in love with it instantly, not least because of the fantastic potential of its garden.

I began to query my motivation for wanting a cottage in the country with the additional responsibility and endless travelling backwards and forwards it would entail and decided to abandon my original idea as unworkable. Instead I would bring the country to my house, open up the fireplaces, banish the stripped pine and transform the garden from a neglected wilderness to the delightful ordered chaos of a country garden. For me, one of the trees most redolent of a country existence is *Magnolia grandiflora*: I used to see it growing by the walls of the grand country houses I visited when I was young, so to see one growing at the front here, even though it had been cut down to a height of only two and a half feet, was another factor in my decision to move here. Association is frequently crucial in establishing the 'right' atmosphere in a house or garden and by identifying positive elements – it may be a plant, a shape, a smell, a colour or a piece of furniture – and introducing them, the ambience of a place can be completely altered.

When I realised that my first house had got too small for me I immediately
began looking to fulfil my dream of a cottage in the country
with a large rambling garden and plenty of space. My obsession with
nature meant I missed living in the country badly and my tiny backyard
in Fulham was scarcely a garden though I crammed it as full of plants
as I could. Honeysuckle, roses and herbaceous perennials were all things
that I associated with a country existence and I longed to be able
to grow. I now have several honeysuckles in the garden, including
this one, fresh from overnight rain.

MAKING AN ENTRANCE

One of the most curious things about the house was that it effectively had two front doors. The one to the left of the house was originally conceived as a back door for use by servants and tradesmen. It gave on to a dark and pokey passage with access to the basement kitchen and led on to the shed at the rear of the house and the garden. It seemed criminal to double up on the space required for an entrance and hallway so I decided to get rid of one of them. There was nothing to be gained from removing the passageway to the left of the house, but much to be gained by taking away the main front door, making a window in its stead and creating an L-shaped sitting room. Outside, rather than demolish the redundant steps leading up to the door, I decided to make a feature of them: by partially building them up with brick to create a trough for planting and liberally covering them with pots their original function is well disguised from all but the most discerning eye. It often pays dividends to consider whether an obsolete feature can be turned to alternative use before getting rid of it: the cost of simulating a like effect at a later stage is usually prohibitive.

Having removed the main front door, the hallway that remained was extremely narrow. To reduce the impression of this I mirrored the walls floor to ceiling both sides and superimposed the wooden gothic arches – painted my favourite green – which echo again and again in the mirrors. To soften the effect I put in the pair of rounded topiary shapes of box – nothing would grow there because it is so gloomy – now turned from fresh green to a golden yellow-green. The terracotta pots go well with the tiles on the floor. Mirrors are a potent decorative tool, their versatility and value much underestimated by modern decorators in both small and large spaces: the French understand them better and the magnificent gallery at Versailles, which relies on mirrors for its spectacular effects, is only the grandest of many exemplars.

My house is typical of the 1880s Victorian style. The twin dormer windows belong to my bedroom, part of the additional storey I had built onto the house before I moved in. The wall, wrought iron railings and gate give me some protection and privacy. The small tree by the bay window is the evergreen *Magnolia grandiflora*, one of the things that first attracted me to the house. It has magnificent creamy-white scented flowers 4–8 inches across from July to September.

The hallway presented me with two major problems: it was small and it was dark. I introduced light through the half-glazed front door and from the other end by installing a large window at the bottom of the stairs. The problem of space was alleviated in part by mirroring the walls. The repeated reflection of the gothic style wooden arches broadens the space laterally while the dried box, clipped to a rounded topiary shape, creates additional interest and picks up a theme established outside.

A PLACE TO ENTERTAIN

It was important to me that the house should lend itself to entertaining. The room or area in which you entertain sets the mood for the occasion and as I enjoy entertaining friends on an intimate as well as, occasionally, on a larger scale I wanted to make sure I had several options to choose from. With the additional space provided by the removal of the hall the sitting-room serves a large gathering for drinks or a small one for dinner excellently. The L-shape of the room means I can readily use only a part of it, changing the shape and emphasis by lighting and the disposition of the furniture. At first the room was carpeted in a good neutral beige, but the room didn't quite work. It wasn't until I went to New York, and chanced to go into a friend's loft that I knew what was wrong. There the floor was bare, the boards bleached, and I knew immediately that the effect would be exactly right for this room. As soon as I got home I had the carpet taken up. The difference was staggering. The whole room opened out, it became larger, more practical – the spilling of wine and the accumulation of dog hairs was no longer a problem – and above all it became more rustic, more me. In due course I may find a rug to break it up a bit, but it suits me well for now.

The drawing-room has a slightly oriental feel created by the low Japanese-style table, the Buddha which I found neglected in a shop in Sri Lanka and the large Tibetan wall-hanging behind the sofa. The coffee-table is ideal for large colourful displays of fresh flowers. Here gorgeous pink and orange lilies, which are among my favourite flowers, are set off by large hydrangea heads and graceful branches of senecio foliage. The informal, loose, countrified yet considered, style of the decoration is one I like very much. Note that the top edge of the container has been hidden by the flowers, and how this contributes to the overall softness.

The size and shape of the room mean it is relatively easy to create quite different decorative effects with flowers, and the pieces of furniture – or permanent props – have been chosen with that in mind. The low marble-topped coffee table acts as a focal point for the short arm of the 'L' and is ideal for splashy, vigorous displays of fresh flowers which attract the attention without dominating the room because of the height at which they are placed. The bay window serves as an alternative focus and allows use of the full height of the room to maximum effect as plants set back within it are automatically prevented from becoming overbearing. The beige drapes and blind are unobtrusive. They avoid potential conflict and provide a neutral backdrop to an infinitely variable range of decorations. If you have furniture or decorations you want to show off it is important not to choose furnishings that will fight with them for attention.

The room changes with the seasons and is sometimes grand, sometimes informal. The mirrors in the alcoves along the wall (which runs from the front to the back of the house, the long arm of the 'L') were installed to enlarge the space still further and to give an unexpected impression of movement. I sometimes have dinner in this room – a round table works well for a small semi-grand party of four people and it looks ravishing with a fire blazing in the grate and candles dancing in the mirrors. But the real joy of having such a large, light room to play with is the opportunity it offers for bringing the garden into the house.

The round table set into the bay window is a good site for showing off the palm tree, which nearly reaches the ceiling. The recess prevents it from dominating that end of the room and smaller plants and the statue all fit comfortably underneath its fronds. The roughly carved bowl, brimful of home-made pot pourri – delphiniums, roses, lavender – introduces a variety of colours and textures. The choice of neutral drapes and walls means that any colour I introduce with floral decorations achieves maximum effect because the contrast is so marked.

Lavender is one of my favourite flowers and one that works in the house particularly well. It is straightforward to dry and *en masse* inside as well as out, it is very effective. It is relatively easy to create topiary-like shapes as I have here because the slightness of the stems allows for gentle gradation. The soft colouring perfectly complements the terracotta urn it is sitting in and its proximity to the fireplace emphasizes the distinctive scent which the heat brings out, a happy reminder of summer in the depths of winter.

The vigorous, vital quality of both these decorations reflects my love of country flowers. In creating a large decoration I am consciously trying to emulate the unfettered joy of nature and here the bright red viburnum berries, tumbling ivy and beech leaves (right), and the arching buddleia, hollyhocks and delphiniums, rambling roses and honeysuckle (above), reflect this. Judiciously placed lilies also help break up the decoration above. The mirror, lining the alcove behind the elegant console table I got from Nancy Lancaster at Colefax, enhances the impression of carefree growth, while the topiary box in its terracotta pot, brought in from outside, blurs the distinction between 'house' and 'garden' that is so rigidly observed by some and which I constantly seek to dissolve.

The garden is really almost a more important part of my home than the house, although I find it unnatural to draw a distinction between the two. Essentially it should be an extension of the house and something you enjoy in its own right as much as the house itself. There should be a little nook where you can curl up with a book, a corner to chat with a friend, a place to serve drinks – in fact an overflow of the house.

The garden here is long for a London garden – 175 feet – and is one of the reasons I wanted this house, but it is also narrow and the way I have laid it out is designed to disguise this defect. The sort of garden where you can see from one end to the other, an uninterrupted expanse of green lawn with the odd tree, bordered on either side with beds, is desperately dull: there should be a framed view wherever you look, and the eye should be offered surprise after surprise. Only the bare bones of the garden – the espalier trees, the damson, the apple and one or two of the roses – were here when I arrived; it was a wilderness, so the design possibilities were legion. I decided to make the most of the length of the garden by creating a series of rooms. In doing this, although the arrangement is necessarily strictly linear, the eye has a new focus every thirty to forty feet; and because one has seen so much one is deceived into thinking that the garden is enormous.

The garden which has made the most lasting impression on me was that of my grandfather. I used to spend a lot of time with him in the holidays and it was he who taught me how to dig, how to weed and how to garden. He gave me a patch of my own to cultivate and would leave a list of instructions of what I was to do while he was out at work. His garden was magical – the house was set on a hill and the whole property was enclosed by enormous stone walls eight to ten feet high. When you got to the top of the hill there was a leather string which, when pulled, opened a door into the garden. A rose arbour led from it to the house and one area of the garden, then there was another door in a wall which led to an orchard and a further door into the kitchen garden – a series of walled gardens within a wall. I loved it – the excitement of never quite knowing what would be behind the next door was tremendous and it is this feeling of excitement and surprise, fundamental to the success of my grandfather's garden, that I have tried to bring to my own garden here.

Busts and urns are among my favourite props and I use them wherever possible both in and out of the house. The head of Hadrian's lover Antonius (left) emerges from a sea of greenery in the pot garden and is set off by a delicate floribunda rose. BELOW The glorious group of roses in pots, brought in from the pot garden, cluster round a bust I was given by friends who were moving, and give the drawing room a summery feel. Here, it is the effect of the roses massed together that make the decoration so spectacular – only one pot would look rather forlorn.

RIGHT The pot garden is at its peak with geraniums and pelargoniums a riot of pinks and reds, sharply contrasted with the soft daisies and rampant New Dawn rose climbing up the fence. Note how the sturdy box have receded into the background in the face of the strong competition from the annuals. LEFT The urn on a pedestal divides the blue and white garden from the herbaceous borders beyond. The standard fuchsia with the variegated ivy reaching down towards it breaks up this cool shady corner.

ESTABLISHING THE GARDEN

TOP LEFT Variegated ivy and an unusual mauve fuchsia tumbling from an urn. Ivy is particularly useful as wall and ground cover. It will grow almost anywhere requiring no sun to thrive, and can make a dramatic contribution to floral decorations, adding an element of mystery.

TOP RIGHT The herbaceous border garden is at its best from June to September. Roses on the fencing panels mingle in with hollyhocks, peonies, polyanthus and nicotiana.

BOTTOM LEFT The strong dark shape of the apple tree shades the table from the fiercest sun. Mauve tulips, ferns, clipped box and helichrysum provide interesting contrasts of colour and texture.

BOTTOM RIGHT The tall slatted fencing panels work extremely well. They provide privacy yet let in the light and the roses I have planted all the way along them do very well.

The garden to the right of mine was a complete jungle when I arrived; an old lady lived there and the garden hadn't been touched for around twenty-five years: there was even a resident fox that I would see from time to time. Then one day I came home to discover that the whole plot had been cleared and my private semi-rural idyll was threatened. There was no problem to the left because the fence is broken up by trees anyway but the excavation to the right meant I now needed a fence. Fences are difficult because they are required to act as an effective barrier without being offensive to the eye: brick walls are aesthetically appealing but they are also extremely expensive, while much of the wooden fencing on the market is unimaginative and has little to recommend it. In the end I designed my own – tall vertical slatted panels over ten feet high and four feet wide, shaped like the template for a gothic arch, picking up an idea I had already used in the house. They were creosoted for protection and to encourage them to weather quickly. I have planted them alternately with roses and ivies, the latter to provide some interest in winter when the roses die back. The plants are still only young – in fact I'm still planting – but I'm already beginning to get the effect I was looking for.

In planning the garden I've tried to be as 'country' as possible – I hate formal planting – and to work the design so it could be enjoyed all the year round. I have something blooming at all times, even in winter, although occasionally freak frosts can frustrate the best endeavours. There are five principal rooms in the garden: the pot garden, the blue and white garden, the border garden, the shrub garden and the vegetable garden.

The blue and white garden, the border garden and the shrub garden are full of plants suitable for fresh displays and for drying. The blue and white garden is a 'walk through' (that is, there's nowhere to sit or for a group of people to stand) where I've planted white roses, ceanothus – a spectacular climbing shrub which carries a cascade of pale blue flowers in summer – white *Clematis montana*, grey foliage supplied by eucalyptus, artemisia, santolina, and in summer I usually put the odd terracotta pot there to give it extra lushness. A pair of huge bay trees mark the entrance to the border garden, and here I have mainly planted herbaceous perennials: delphiniums, foxgloves, peonies, hellebores for spring and of course roses on the panels and climbing up through the branches of the apple tree – a traditionally English, attractive combination – though I do put in some cottage-style bedding plants (nicotiana, cosmos, zinnias) in the summer. Then in the shrub garden there are more roses – soft pink New Dawn, Constance Spry in the pear tree – deutzia, rhododenrons, azaleas, camellias and a *Viburnum fragrans* which, as its name suggests, is sweetly scented and provides a delicate splash of colour in the dark winter months. At the far end of the garden a row of x. *Cupressus leylandii* divide the pleasure garden from the working garden and hide the unsightly greenhouse and shed. I grow spinach, broad beans, peas, carrots, blackberries, red and black currants; the pleasure of eating home-grown fruit and vegetables more than justifies the space taken from the flower garden.

Hogweed is one of the most architecturally striking plants in the garden. *Heracleum mantegazzianum* can grow to a height of some ten feet and prefers a shady, slightly damp sheltered spot. The foliage is spectacular: vast toothy leaves anything up to a maximum of three feet long grow from a substantial, poisonous, prickly stem that can cause severe skin irritation. The plant will grow well indoors if kept out of direct sunlight and immediately dramatizes a gloomy corner. I brought it in at first because the shadows fascinated me and then found that abandoned in the corner, it dried beautifully to a crisp, golden perfection, the seed heads captured at their most fairy-like.

As well as being decorative in its own right, the garden is of course a fantastic source of inspiration, ideas and materials for decorating the house. The pot garden works particularly well in this respect. I grow the lilies and roses there for the house, especially for the drawing room, and even before I moved in I managed to persuade the previous occupier to let me plant some lilies so that when I arrived in June the garden would not be bare and colourless. Although I sometimes do set-piece decorations with fresh flowers, especially if I am entertaining, I tend to prefer the more chaotic effect created by bringing things like terracotta pots and urns into the house.

One of my favourite things in the garden is the hogweed. It is extremely poisonous and skin contact with its stem and leaves causes a vicious rash – but it is worth the risk for the splendour of its size and shape. It can be used to fill a dreary corner in the house or garden and will create fantastic patterns and shadows on the ceiling with up-lighters. The other advantage is that you can make a semi-permanent decorative feature of it as it will last for years and is equally spectacular alive or dead – it dries excellently. But be careful if you plant hogweed in the garden as it is invasive and once established will readily take over a small garden completely.

POT POURRI

Like the hogweed much of the herbaceous content of the garden lends itself well to drying, and if you like dried flowers and have the space to dry them yourself it is worth growing certain flowers especially for this purpose. Pot pourri is also easy to make and can be used effectively all over the house both for its decorative effect and for its pleasant scent. The method I use creates a rough-style dramatic pot pourri which suits me and the style of the house. When shrubs, roses and the herbaceous plants have almost finished flowering I go round the garden with a basket, snapping off and collecting my favourite flower heads. The mix will depend on my mood and what's available at the time. I allow them to dry out then heap them into a large bowl with the most interesting heads on top and add floral essence 'to taste'. I usually use one of my

Peonies are among the richest of herbaceous plants, with their large showy flowers and appealing foliage. Suitable for inclusion in a herbaceous, mixed or shrub border, they can take some time to become established and dislike being disturbed, but once settled they will provide superb blooms, excellent for cutting and good for drying.

own, a range developed from scents I have discovered on walks or in the garden, and these and many others are obtainable in herbal shops and department stores. The essence can be used to bring out the scents of the flowers you have picked (lavender, for instance) or introduce additional fragrances, perhaps a blend of several flowers. When the scent fades you can renew it by adding a few more drops of essence.

Scents or smells play a surprisingly large part in establishing a mood or ambience. Usually we don't notice them unless they are particularly strong – whether pleasant or disagreeable – but they work away in our subconsious and their contribution in invoking a memory or association has been well proven: roses, jasmine, lavender recall the fresh, heady days of summer, while cedar, pine cones and wood smoke evoke the darkness and cosiness of autumn and winter. They are therefore important as a background to the statement you are trying to make with your decorative scheme and you should think of smell as an integral part of it.

The rich blowsy peony flowers really come into their own in this dried decoration, their size requiring more than half a dozen rosebuds to balance each one. The soft pinks contrast happily with the sprigs of lavender and waves of alchemilla mollis and eucalyptus. The glass cylinder filled to the brim with pot pourri is an unusual way to show off the different textures and colours of the flowers and petals pushed against the side. Similar, striking effects can be achieved with pebbles and shells.

A BASEMENT
KITCHEN

My prime concern when deciding how to treat the kitchen was the need to create a room that was not only functional but also suitable for entertaining as there was no space in the house for a separate dining room. The existing kitchen area was located in the basement, reached by stairs from the hallway, with another room used as a utility room-cum-scullery adjacent to it. My original plan was to open up the space, including the stairs, entirely. I did have the partition between the two rooms taken away but building regulations meant I was obliged to leave the stairs boxed in. I am actually quite glad of it now because it allows the room to be far cosier. I suspect that in winter it would have made the room very drafty and certainly the people sitting by the stairs would have been very exposed.

The kitchen table (which originally came from the Duke and Duchess of Devonshire's old house in Cheyne Walk) used to be in the old shop in Avery Row where it did sterling service as a planting-up table. It now seats eight comfortably for dinner and doesn't need the degree of care that a good mahogany table might, allowing me to create miniature gardens like this one on it as a centrepiece. The moss acts as a pleasing diguise to the containers holding the herbs and frequently comes in extremely useful in this respect. I grow a lot of herbs in the garden, in pots and in the borders, although I don't have a herb garden as such. Here you can see pineapple mint, basil, parsley, catmint, bergamot, chives and thyme.

My quest for a 'country house' inevitably led me to a natural range of wooden kitchen units that could also be used to display my mixed collection of china. The fridge has been disguised behind panel doors so it intrudes as little as possible. The terracotta tiles on the work surface, followed through to the splash back, and the crude wooden chopping boards and fruit and vegetable bowls all contribute to the rustic feel that I was seeking to achieve. The strings of peppers, chillis and garlic, the pots of herbs and the bunches of herbs tucked in along the top of the units – marjoram, sweet bay, santolina, sage, lavender, thyme, poppy heads – all help create a homely inviting environment.

I consciously rejected all the overtly 'kitcheny' and modern, hi-tech, designs that are much in fashion, as above all I wanted the kitchen to be cosy and inviting, continuing my country house theme, and my choice of sturdy, natural wood units, rich red fabric for the sofa, warm colourful rugs and homely collections of herbs and china were all designed to reflect this. The idea of bringing my guests downstairs to a roaring fire, comfortable sofa and pre-prandial drink really appealed to me and so I made it possible. It was surprising and it

was also extremely practical. There was no danger of neglecting my guests while I was cooking because I could chat to them from where I was working, they could enjoy the blazing fire and I could simply bring the casserole or whatever to the table when we were ready. Alternatively, we could have drinks in the sitting room and then come downstairs for dinner, or start in the garden and come in via the pot garden, down the steps through the French windows (a feature I was pleased to find *in situ* when I arrived).

This round table, tucked into the corner between the fireplace and the bay window facing the street, is a haven for my collection of porcelain figurines and copperware. The jug of bright pink allium in front of the rye grass defines the left hand edge, opposed on the right by a glorious group of pink and red roses. In between, pansies jostle with petunias and more roses, creating an image similar to the traditional cottage garden; the two candelabra at the rear introduce a note of romance so that one half expects the figures to get up and dance. The window seat, just visible to the right, runs all the way round the bay window, and acts as a useful storage area.

The kitchen table runs parallel to the units with French windows leading out to the garden at one end. The proximity of the work surface is a bonus for serving meals and with the candles lit on the table and the sub-pelmet lights extinguished one hardly remembers one is in a kitchen at all. For an instant table decoration requiring little thought and planning, pots of flowers linked with trails of ivy can look stunning. A similar effect could be achieved with any number of plants – spring bulbs like narcissi, lilies, winter jasmine, all of which are readily available in the proper season. Alternatively you could create an attractive still life with fruit and vegetables.

The blue and white plates are a good example of my magpie habits: I have collected them over a number of years on holidays in England, Scotland and Ireland; now they are much more difficult to find. The pair of sculptures in the weathered urns on the old flour bin found in a junk shop is made from dried celosia flowers. Over the years they have mellowed from a strong dark red to this burnished orange, which actually suits my colour scheme better. See how the humpy texture of the moss at the base of the stem reflects the look of the sculpture head. Celosia is an annual species and the plants are best grown under glass.

If I am entertaining in the kitchen I will always do something to dress up the room or the table, however simple. Decoration is an indication of the regard you have for your guests, an additional attention to give them pleasure, a subtle form of flattery. If I'm short of time, it may be that I will simply rush into the garden and pick some flowers, fruit or vegetables, or bring in some pots of herbs, bulbs, roses or whatever is available to put on the table as a diversion. It doesn't matter what it is as long as you like it and it is what *you* want to do. The wonderful thing about decoration is that it is essentially self-indulgent, by definition designed to please its creator as much as any on-looker. There is certainly no need to produce a contrived floral decoration for the table unless that is what you want, and personally, especially for the kitchen, the more rustic the effect the better I like it. Sometimes of course one does have the time (and the inclination) to plan a whole decorative scheme for the table but on those occasions when one does not it is important to realize that the most successful hosts live by their own rules and are not troubled by anybody else's.

The large inviting sofa facing the open fireplace is one of the key elements in creating a warm, welcoming, cosy kitchen. Guests can sit here while I'm preparing supper at the range to the right and help themselves to drinks from the butler's tray if my hands are occupied. The lacquer lamps (there are two) I found in Scotland and there is more blue and white china in the dresser.

As you walk down the path outside leading to the front door you see two small square windows packed with colour. These are the two large displays of dried flowers seen here, from the kitchen side apparently nestling in alcoves rather than on a window ledge. There is an eclectic mix of colour and texture – buddleia, hydrangea, peonies, roses, achillea, physalis and the emphatic hogweed. The greenery, which adds to the impression of a 'living' arrangement, has been coated with glycerine to preserve it. The effect of these two eye-catching decorations is to make this half of the kitchen work as a room in its own right, so that it is easy to forget that all the more usual trappings of a kitchen are just out of view.

CREATING A GARDEN ROOM

My success in creating exactly my ideal kitchen meant that I was left without an area for more formal entertaining, particularly dinner parties for more than four people. The idea of a conservatory or garden room has always attracted me, primarily because it seemed to epitomize my idea of the garden as an extension of the house. The distinction between the two becomes even more blurred in an area whose first aim is to house plants and to provide protection for those species not hardy enough to survive Britain's temperate climate. The only place where it was feasible for me to build a conservatory was as an extension sideways from the passage that led from the front door to the flower room. Apart from not taking light from any existing windows, this location had the additional advantage of making the flower room more of a unit with the house. The gothic-style arches of the frames in the conservatory, carried through to a pattern superimposed on the completely mirrored walls, reflected what I had already done in the hallway (which now leads directly into this room) and on to the flower room, which also has gothic windows and which I use for storing crockery, bas-

kets, boots and dejected plants on their way to the greenhouse or garden shed. In the garden room the mirrors again increase the impression of size and, with the fleshy foliage of the plants reflected in them, in daylight the room has the opaque quality of the tropical rain forest, and at night, by candlelight, it is quite other-worldly. A frequent problem of conservatories is glare: here the roof is half tiled and half glazed, designed so that when the sun comes round in the latter part of the day there is no need for blinds for protection from it.

BELOW Chairs dressed in a simple terracotta printed fabric strike a warmer note picked up by the colourful chilli peppers sprouting from the central decoration. The large basket, with smaller panniers overflowing with fruit, creates a cornucopia-like effect, while the senses are further stimulated by the inclusion of herbs – long stems of rosemary and parsley. The whole is given height and space to breathe by the volcanic eruption of variegated grasses and cow's parsley.

The garden room, or conservatory, which I built on to the house to create an area for more formal entertaining – especially dinner parties – I have made into a small sub-tropical oasis. I have filled it with bamboo, orange trees, *Ficus benjamina* and shlefera, all a good height to start with; their reflection in the mirror increases the jungly effect. White, wooden, slatted, garden chairs surround a comparatively (for me) formally dresssed dinner table. The Herend china looks well with the restrained centrepiece made from artichokes, cabbages, moss and bright red roses; note how the choice of napkin brings out their colour.

49

The garden room works exceptionally well for dinner parties and guests love its dramatic, slightly exotic, quality. If it's just too cold to eat outside we can be in there with the doors open and the difference is negligible. In summer sweet rich scents from the pot garden – jasmine, nicotiana, night-scented stock, planted specially for the purpose – waft through the door and crickets chirp noisily so it is easy to imagine oneself on some Mediterranean verandah. The room is practical too: there are two cupboards hidden in the walls which I use for storing glasses, and food can be brought out of the kitchen via the French windows and the terrace rather than negotiating the somewhat awkward steps inside the house. The terracotta tiled floor (the same tiles as in the hall) keeps the room beautifully cool, though there are radiators hidden behind panels if I want to warm it up in winter. The room is easy to decorate as the framework is here already. The side-table makes a perfect setting for a splash of colour and it is fun to play up the tropical effect with a display of colourful exotic fruits and vegetables.

Eating outside is a great pleasure and is done more often and more stylishly by almost every other nation than Britain (the only exception is the picnic, which the British do best), and it seems to me criminal not to make the most of every available opportunity to be outside and to enjoy the garden on the glorious sunny days that we are given. I have deliberately created several areas in the garden where it is possible to eat comfortably. The pot garden benefits from the exterior lighting and its proximity to the house for a more elaborate meal and barbecues are easy there with the York stone firm underfoot. In the pot garden, the area under the apple tree – an old variety of Charles Greaves, nearly a hundred years old, with Albertine, New Dawn, *Clematis montana* and honeysuckle growing up through its branches – is my favourite spot in the whole garden for dining out on a summer's evening. Although the back of the house faces north-west, most of the garden gets sun for much of the day because of its length.

Taken from an upstairs window before the garden room was built, this photograph gives a very good idea of the open situation of the house, with playing fields beyond, but also of the narrowness of the garden, which from ground level I have done all I can to disguise. On a warm clear summer's evening entertaining outside is one of life's great pleasures. Lit by exterior spotlights which only succeed in making pools of light in the gloom, and by traditional hurricane lamps on the table, the garden takes on an aura of magic. Surrounded by sweet scents, trailing greenery and the riches of my pot garden a table decoration as such almost becomes redundant. I might, however, place a pot of night-scented stocks near each chair, clothe the table in moss or make rustic candlesticks from artichokes, cabbages, celery or birch.

Spring is one of my favourite times of year. The whole earth seems to come alive, with buds bursting, birds singing and building their nests, new shoots thrusting up through the earth, delicate pale green leaves and magnificent light feathery blossom signalling the passing of winter. The garden is a delight with discoveries to be made every day of a new shoot or cluster of bulbs in flower, only overshadowed by the threat of savage frost which can catch the unwary as late as May.

As the bulbs – daffodils, tulips, irises, narcissi – start to flood the market (usually slightly ahead of the garden) and foliage is renewed on bare branches, decorating with fresh flowers seems almost obligatory and the strengthening sun begins to brighten rooms to the point where they almost demand a spring posy or display.

The sight of this old apple tree in blossom is one of the greatest delights of spring. The old horse-shoe seat, which my mother encouraged me to buy in a junk shop we passed in the road, makes an idyllic arbour beneath it. The discarded white petals scattered on the grass and the neighbouring giant hogweed leaves, waiting like plates to catch them, are an attractive, unplanned, bonus. It is the perfect place to enjoy a leisurely breakfast on a warm sunny, Sunday morning.

MY MOTHER'S BEDROOM

When I first came here my mother was the most important guest who was likely to stay, so I wanted to create a suite of rooms that she would take particular pleasure in. Spring colours were her favourites – soft yellows, pinks and pale greens – and she loved blowsy chintzes so it was only a question of searching out a fabric which combined all the necessary elements. They are good colours anyway for a bedroom, which ought to be restful and relaxing yet inspiring when you wake in the morning.

The room is not particularly large, although it comfortably houses the four-

on the four-poster successfully evokes images of spring and summer gardens. The walls and window drapes continue the pale yellow theme, allowing the main colour contrast in the room, the green lining of the bed drapes, again to focus attention on the bed. Other furniture in the room has been kept to a minimum, while the pictures maintain

poster bed (on the wall furthest from the door) which is presented as the focal point, and has a pair of standard sash windows looking out on to the road. The fact that the room doesn't have a garden view was another reason for wanting to introduce a floral fabric, and the one I eventually chose for the drapes

the soft romantic mood that has been established by the colour scheme. The room is an excellent example of how straightforward and ultimately successful the decorative process can be if you first think through what you are trying to achieve and consistently pursue that goal.

LEFT Quite different moods are created by the two treatments of the right-hand
bedside table. The pink miniature roses grouped in pots in a brass bowl are far
more restrained than the exuberant display of fresh flowers, where the predominant
colour is still pink. Hydrangea heads, roses, dianthus are perfectly set off by the broad-
leaved hostas and silvery fern. The gorgeously rich-coloured basket of drieds, set
on the floor underneath the roses, could equally well have replaced them, and in
winter would create a satisfying reminder of summer.

ABOVE Daisies, alchemilla mollis, helichrysum
and variegated pelargonium leaves cluster
with glorious white philadelphus flowers in
the pretty feminine porcelain vase. Behind,
a semi-permanent decoration of dried
flowers crowning a cylinder of pot pourri is
muted by contrast with the fresh.

Although the bathroom is not actually adjacent to the bedroom there was no reason not to treat them as a unit for decorative purposes. The bathroom itself is tiny, occupying the space over the hallway and has a window to front and back. It is just wide enough to put a bath widthways across the room, so I did this, installing it about a foot out from the end wall to leave space for a decent shelf. I decided to use the same floral fabric as had been used on the four poster in the bedroom for the walls and ceiling as well as the windows, trimming the corners and edges with a toning creamy yellow brocade. The white panelling to dado height prevents the overall effect from being oppressive and demonstrates that it is possible to use a large pattern in a confined space as long as this is done with care.

The foot-wide shelf between the bath and the outside wall gives just enough space to display a collection of natural sponges (from Turkey) and some spectacular shells. Pressed for space in this small bathroom, the mirrors behind the bath at least give an impression of greater depth, while the satin finish of the fabric and the gold fittings on the bath give the room an air of luxury despite its size, that chrome fittings and a plain cotton would never have achieved.

RIGHT Even the wc has been boxed in in sympathy with the white panelling below the dado rail and to create another valuable surface. On it the musicians wait in vain for the nod from the conductor, the empty heads of the white cherubs have been filled with a mass of dried flowers, while the dried lavender in the china basket on the right exudes its familiar scent. In spring, bulbs – lily of the valley, snowdrops, narcissi, hyacinths – all do well here, fed by the light from the window to the back of the house.

THE MASTER BEDROOM

My bedroom, which is situated right at the top of the house, simply did not exist when I came here. I took the roof off the house and had the top storey built on before I moved in to create a sizeable bedroom and bathroom suite for myself; the folding double doors between the two give an extra dimension when open. The bathroom is like paradise. I can lie back in the bath surrounded by all the overhanging foliage, dream of foreign places and watch a game of cricket on the common beyond the garden. I deliberately sited the bath in the centre of the room in front of the window as there was no pressure on space forcing me to put it against a wall. The French complain that the English always range furniture round the edge of rooms rather than making the most of the central space and I tend to think they are right. The main point of the room is the bath, so it seemed rather senseless to push it to one side as though it were an embarrassment.

The bedroom itself has a very modern, hi-tech, streak unrepresented in the rest of the house. The contrast of the brickwork, left bare on the party wall like the interior of an old barn, with the upright steel struts of the bed appeals to a side of my nature that doesn't usually get a chance to express itself. The bed itself is, of course, a glorious combination of old and new: the frame bed is a very traditional idea, but to realize it in metal is very modern. Eventually I will probably acquire a genuine four poster bed, but this one is fine meanwhile. Occasionally clients give me the opportunity to experiment with really modern, avant-garde ideas, but, except in this room, they are not really appropriate for this house and what I'm aiming to achieve.

LEFT Siting the bath centrally meant that I could surround it on three sides with foliage. The large window and humid atmosphere allow sub-tropical plants like a date palm (*Phoenix dactylifera*), *Dracaena deremensis* and *Ficus lyrata* to thrive in their wicker baskets and urns. Even the winter jasmine (*Jasminum polyanthum*) by the window seems to enjoy being there, despite normally resenting changes in temperature. The marble topped column capital at the end of the bath makes an excellent table.

ABOVE The slope of the roof, mirrored to add interest, reflects an exotic jumble of shells and greenery. The glass cylinder filled with shells resting on a sandy base, presents a fascinating tableau of shape and colour. It could be varied using all one type of shell – cockles, limpets or even dried sea horses – the textural effects are fabulous, just as they are on the accretion of shells above the cylinder. The shell basket, lined with cowries, is intended to be purely decorative, but could be used to house a small sponge or nailbrush.

My bedroom is the only place in the house where there is a decidely 'modern' element. As a rule I prefer the old, the well-used and the traditional, merely combining them in unusual ways. But here having decided to leave the brickwork bare on the chimney-breast, a modern statement seemed appropriate. I change the mood of the room with the seasons – in spring for instance, the blue and white bed coverings are discarded in favour of crisp white Irish linen and the trumpet-blowing angels will be put away until the next autumn. The pair of beautiful panelled mirrors is French as is the sofa in front of the bed. The old Irish console table to the left and the dark marble-topped table to the right of the bed are home to my collection of ginger jars and are ideal for the sizeable but compact decoration of dried flowers shown here, which contrasts attractively with the blue and white china. The bedroom is *ensuite* with the bathroom in a very real sense: the large folding double doors allow palm fronds to reach over towards the bed and are casually reflected in the mirror as though it were nothing unusual.

MAKING AN EXIT

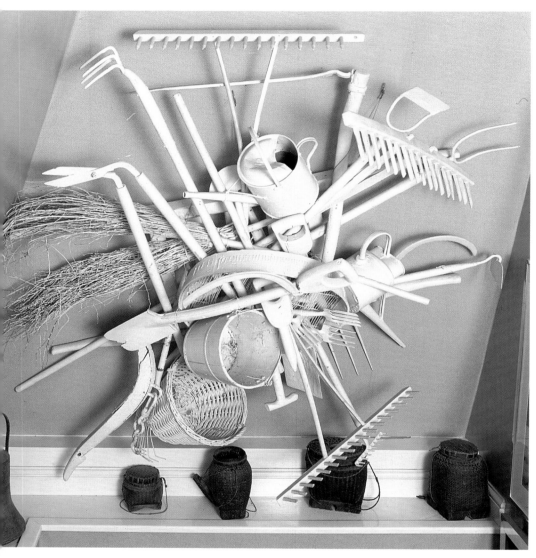

Attention to detail is one of the most important factors in any successful decorative scheme, whatever the scale, and in a house it is the stairs and passages that are frequently neglected. In this house as in many others, there is a blank sloping wall at the top of the stairwell, which is seen by anybody going down stairs: it is therefore ideal for a large and imposing semi-permanent decoration. The 'trophy' – a sculpture based on the use of traditional agricultural and garden tools – is an idea I first had ten years ago and which I have used in a variety of ways since. The join between the wall and the roof slope also seemed ripe for exploitation; there are rarely enough horizontal surfaces for display in a house, so I decided to make the most of the opportunity and put in a wide shelf. I can add to the permanent collection I keep there with a decoration of lavender or other dried flowers.

There is often a deceptive amount of space on half-landings in a house as I discovered when I was trying to find a home for an elegant marble-topped table that used to be in the shop. The emptiness beneath the pictures there had always bothered me and now not only do I have the table comfortably nestling against the wall, it also presents an opportunity for decoration. Dark at the best of times, I was anxious to bring as much light into the hall and stairs as possible. The most practical solution was to put in a large window overlooking the garden at the bottom of the stair well, and this I did. It gave the added bonus of allowing me to put a large plant at the foot of the well on the deep window ledge, which otherwise would not have been possible.

The 'trophy' sculpture is in many ways my homage to nature. Made up of traditional agricultural and garden tools – rakes, hoes, besoms, pitchforks, scythes, sickles, pails, baskets, watering-cans and a plough-share – it symbolizes man's attempts to come to terms with nature. Painted white to stand out from the mottled green wallpaper I see it most days of my life first thing in the morning and last thing at night; it acts as a constant reminder of – and as a silent prayer of thanks for – what nature can and has given to me.

RIGHT The arrival of the table on the half-landing outside the drawing room allowed me to make an emphatic statement even before entering the room itself. The twin urns and small ethnic African sculptures – smooth, rounded, figures – represent the marriage of two quite alien cultures. From the urns sprout birch twigs nearly three times their height, reaching almost to the ceiling. At the base of the twigs moss provides a bed for mixture of dried petals and fruits, scattered like an offering to the gods.

The pot garden at the front of the house is just an echo of the one immediately to the rear of the house, reached through the garden room or the kitchen. There used to be an ugly biscuit-coloured patio of crazy paving at the back and at the front which was quite out of tune with the country house feel. Wanting to keep paving of sorts, I had it taken up and the much more majestic York stone put down instead. It is much more expensive but its good earthy colour and attraction for mosses make it infinitely preferable. In the pot garden to the rear, apart from the plants with scented flowers, there are usually lilies, roses and hardy camellias for use in and out of the house, and of course the topiaries of clipped box. I love topiary for its severity and for its form-

ality but also for its flexibility – one of the box is clipped into the shape of a fox. In winter the evergreens create some interest when other things have died back and the architectural shapes of the topiary give the garden some form.

At the front I eventually want to walk through a tunnel of vegetation to get to or from the house. I had the arches and the wrought iron gate put in and the plants are slowly growing up over them. Already I feel as though I am entering a different world when I enter my home because of what I have created here. My attachment to this house is tremendously strong: I feel part of the bricks and mortar and I want the way in and out of the house itself to demonstrate clearly that this is a separate world, my world, even to the casual visitor.

The collection of terracotta pots both to the front and to the back of the house gives a sense of unity and completion to the exterior. The gentle formality acts as a caveat to the visitor as they mark the edge of my 'territory', at the same time hinting at what is to come. In time the arches at the front will be entirely grown over with ivies, white roses and a riot of clematis montana, romantic and intriguing to some, gloomy, claustrophobic and intimidating to others.

THE FRUITS

OF THE

EARTH

DRIED FLOWERS

The acceptance and growth of the use of dried flowers is the single most important development in the flower industry in the last decade. Few flower shops would now be without them, and in addition they have helped bring flowers to a wider public through non-traditional outlets such as department stores. The same niche in the market was aimed at by the manufacturers of silk flowers but although they are still widely available, they were too expensive and not realistic enough and so never took off in the same way.

When I started in the business the range of dried flowers available was astonishingly limited: there was no colour, only dreary beiges and whites that were as uninspiring as they were unimaginative; the most exciting product you could get hold of was bull rushes. Like everyone else I would have fresh flowers in my home. One day, however, I suddenly noticed some delphiniums I had forgotten in a dark corner, and realized that they had dried perfectly. And if delphiniums would dry, why not a whole host of herbaceous and other plants? Gradually the potential percolated through to the growers as demand from decorators like myself increased. Little by little the full range of herbaceous – delphiniums, peonies, hydrangea, larkspur – roses and grasses, rich in variety of colour and texture, become available. The dried flower scene was revolutionized, encouraging experimentation and the development of new ideas.

ABOVE Baskets, terracotta pots, scented candles and dried flowers all work well together, in any combination. Autumnal in spirit, this wreath of wheat, physalis, poppy heads, allium and roses placed round the multi-wicked candle would make a simple yet attractive table decoration. The heat of the tiny flames encourages the dried flowers to give off their residual scent, mingling with that from the candle.

RIGHT I buy all my drieds direct from specialist growers like Christine Corson who runs a farm in Godalming. The flowers are hung upside down from chicken wire in a large brick-built out-house to dry. Here there are marigolds, dahlias, zinnias, amaranthus, thistles, achillea, and grasses – to name only a few. She is checking that the flower heads have dried out completely before taking them down.

OVERLEAF Helichrysum, dahlias, statice and gypsophila hanging up to dry at Sue Nicholls' home in Malvern.

Baskets are a particularly effective way of presenting dried flowers. You can vary the style and the approach according to the basket you have and the materials you want to use. Sometimes simplicity works best: these roses look spectacular in the open basket bound with raffia, peeking out from the sides as well as the top. More traditionally, the medium-sized basket has the flowers clustered around the edge, effectively in bunches, with lavender sprays either end of the handle to enliven it.

The value of dried flowers is of course primarily that they last. There is no need to buy new flowers each week as a decoration will last several years or until you are bored of it. The colours do fade and mellow after a while, but the effect is comparable to maturing and ripening rather than degenerating. Drieds cost very little more than fresh flowers these days and if, like me, you have a passion for lilies, probably considerably less. The savings possible over a long period are remarkable. But the attraction of dried flowers today is not so much that they save money as

time. Not only do you save the time spent each week creating a fresh decoration, it is also increasingly easy to buy a ready made dried decoration to suit your needs if you have neither the time nor the inclination to create your own.

However, if you do want to create your own decorations dried flowers are extraordinarily flexible and you can do with them at least as much if not more than with fresh flowers. At the most basic level, for instance, for any degree of permanence fresh flowers have to be kept watered; as drieds do not, you can use them in more unusual ways, wired

in horizontally or hung upside down for instance, without pause for thought. They are ideal for use in baskets and drops for the same reason. The only disadvantage is that you tend to have to use more dried flowers than you would fresh in a decoration, although using materials like moss, catmint or chamomile to pad out the base helps reduce this problem as well as making the base more secure.

Creating a dried flower decoration is comparable to painting a still-life picture because one dimension has been removed; the flowers look vibrant, alive,

To create a similar effect, apart from the basket and the flowers, you will need several lengths of florists' wire to attach the bunches of flowers to the basket, moss or fabric to line it with and needle and thread to bind the fabric to the basket. You could also bind the handle of the basket with the lining for a softer look. Baskets of flowers look attractive on side tables in any room, but are particularly useful in halls and guest-rooms as long as you adapt the colour balance to suit. You can add an extra dimension by filling the centre with pot pourri. Baskets also make an extravagant gift-wrapping, comfortably housing bottles, cakes, china and a host of other gifts.

yet are not. The flower paintings of the Dutch artist Jan Brueghel represent the pinnacle of achievement in this respect and are a constant inspiration to greater endeavour. The aim in decorating with dried flowers is the same as with fresh – maintain a feeling of movement, vitality and surprise by careful selection and juxtaposition. If you're using big, herbaceous-type flowers in a large container you should try to get as natural an effect as possible, as though the flowers were still growing, not arranged; in small decorations, as in large, you should be conscious of colour

grouping and of creating a softness, not just arbitrarily including the nearest stem that comes to hand. Most of the smaller drieds are more effective when used together; singly their delicacy means they don't get much chance to make an impact.

Drying flowers for use in the home is much less trouble than one might expect and can give additional pleasure to the gardener who otherwise labours to produce perfect blooms only for a very short season. If you don't have a garden, suitable plants can be grown in pots and window boxes, picked from hedgerows

and even bought from a flower seller if the quality is right. The most crucial factor in successful drying is ensuring that the flowers are picked at the right time. Most herbaceous flowers should be picked at or just before their peak, when the sap is rising, and certainly before there is the slightest hint that a bloom is dropping or in any way past its best. It's better to pick a flower when it's dry, but if you can't wait or the rain looks set to ruin it, gently shake it to remove any surplus water, then leave the stem in water until the last drops of moisture have evaporated.

This is one of the drying rooms of another of my suppliers, Sue Nicholls, who is based in Malvern. Hanging, from the back, are delphiniums, solidago (golden rod), larkspur and helichrysum. In the containers on the floor by the window are astilbe, molucella, more delphiniums, yellow curry plant, orange physalis and yellow achillea to the rear. The pretty variegated foliage is hornbeam.

It looks as though the flowers in this decoration are actually growing in this unusually shaped, woven, reed basket, an effect that I was consciously seeking to create. The tones are muted but the textures involved are extraordinary. The fragile, slightly crinkled physalis, the rough eared wheat, the smooth lobes of the artichoke, the multi-faceted hydrangea heads and smaller hellebore and the long thin, empty bean pods are all protecting the giant apple made from grasses. The group of hellebore stems reaching to the ground provides the surprise element.

There are several methods of drying and preserving flowers – with glycerine (especially for foliage), with desiccants, pressing – but the easiest and most familiar method is by hanging the flower or seedhead upside down, suspended from a hook or cross-beam. Larger flowers (for example, peonies or artichokes) are best dried individually to avoid damage by crushing, but smaller flowers or foliage (most herbs, lavender, polygonum – knotweed, for instance) may be tied together in bunches, although if you're using some sort of string rather than an elastic band you should be careful that the fixing doesn't become too loose. The ideal environment for drying flowers is warm and dark – attics, airing cupboards, cellars, sheds, the corner of an unused room where curtains can be drawn to minimize light will all do – but the primary requirement is of course that the atmosphere is completely dry and well-ventilated. Warmth helps because the quicker the flower dries, the less time it has to deteriorate before drying, while darkness helps prevent the colours from fading. Drying time varies from flower to flower and experience is the best guide, but do make sure the flower is dry right up to the head which is generally the last place to dry out. Some flowers – for example amaranthus (loves lies bleeding), solidago, astilbe – dry better stood upright in a container with a little water in the bottom which should not be topped up; this preserves the flower-head or stem better than if they were hung upside down, but otherwise the ideal conditions are the same.

The weave of this beautifully crafted basket perfectly complements the tapestry effect of this rich, dense decoration. The flowers are used like strands of different coloured wools, the stitches of each carefully grouped and placed according to a pre-established pattern. This decoration clearly demonstrates the effectiveness and desirability of grouping smaller dried flowers together.

OVERLEAF The interest in this basket of drieds principally derives from the crude rustic handle, crafted from a branch of gnarled thorn.

Dampness is the prime enemy of dried flowers, both during the drying process and in storage or use. If not kept in dry conditions they soon begin to look bedraggled and limp, so avoid using them in the bathroom or hanging them just above the cooker or kettle in the kitchen.

Some flowers require a considerable degree of skill to dry successfully, which can only be acquired by experience, but the vast majority should present the beginner with few problems as long as the precepts outlined above are followed. Some flowers or varieties of flower (certain chrysanthemums, for instance) will not dry at all; specialist books indicate some of them, common sense suggests others, but the best way of finding out is trial and error. Dried flowers have been the salvation of the lean winter months and the gloomy corner; decorating with them an opportunity for experimentation away from the constraints of working with fresh flowers. Drying your own is an additional pleasure, giving a whole new dimension to the planning, creation and care of your garden.

This glorious harvest sheaf (photographed in the shop in Brook Street) would look magnificent in a hallway or set into an empty fireplace. Inspired by traditional stooks of corn, it occurred to me to treat other flowers in the same way. The soft, golden colours of achillea, marigolds, and grasses seemed appropriate to harvest time, while the wheat itself, effectively disguising the container, is used as a decorative border all the way round. The plaited raffia is reminiscent of an old-fashioned corn dolly, while the large stylish bow gives the whole decoration a festive air.

This small compact sculpture, made in the topiary style, is typical of its kind. The pom-pom has been made from the evergreen cupressa and clipped into shape. The stem has been created from young, thin, pliable birch twigs with a hint of red in them; the lateral binding adds to the interest, while the moss at the base balances the greenery at the top.

THE NATURAL WORLD

Following hard on the innovation and development of the use of dried flowers came the realization that there was no need to stop there: nature provides a whole host of materials that can be used for decorating and for creating rather more unusual effects. Nature herself is like some giant collage from which we freely plunder ideas and materials and is unparalleled as a source of inspiration. Decorating with flowers is undoubtedly an art, and a decoration comparable to a painting, where composition and content have been carefully thought out, sometimes with a preliminary sketch. Nature's palette is infinitely variable: among the first materials to find favour with decorators was moss, initially introduced to bring a little green into the house with the dried flowers, but now used as a decorative material in its own right. There are several different sorts of moss available to the decorator and they have different uses according to their appearance and flexibility. There is carpet moss used for trees, bows, baskets and topiaries; bun moss for trees and sculptures, like teddy bears; lichen moss for trees and pyramids; and spaghnum moss which is used mainly as a covering in pots and baskets, and looks particularly effective lining a glass bowl or made into a rustic candlestick.

The development of the sculpture as a medium for decorating with flowers has only taken place in the last few years, although its use is now quite common among leading decorators. I first turned to sculpture in response to an unspoken growth in demand from clients for a decoration that was more an integral part of the home – part of the furniture, so to speak – rather than ephemeral as many strictly floral decorations are. The development of dried flowers made the progression that much easier, because already the massed grouping of some drieds – lavender, for instance – was beginning to look sculptural in form.

This exciting spiky sculpture is made entirely from a mass of magnolia leaves. The shiny upper sides of the leaves catch the light and create interesting shadows of remarkable depth on the multi-faceted surface. Although the leaves are evergreen, untreated they would not last long severed from the tree; therefore they have been coated with glycerine to preserve them.

This photograph hints at the vast range of materials available to the decorator. In the foreground to the left is a magnificent, three-tiered, lichen sculpture nearly six feet tall. Constructed on the same principles as the other, simpler ones, it is a good example of how a lively imagination can develop an idea: in this instance from the single to the multi-tiered sculpture. In addition to its fantastic shape, the lichen itself introduces an element of mystery, with its ghostly colouring and tiny tendrils clumped into knuckles. Behind this sculpture is a tree made from bun moss, while the statue acts as a foil to the burgeoning, calciferous, shell drop.

The idea of the first sculptures was very closely allied to topiary, and topiary shapes continue to be a preoccupation, mainly because of the immense, almost limitless, variety they offer. If you are sculpturing a tree it doesn't have to be a ball, it can be any shape you like: an oval, a mushroom, a mound, a cone, multi-layered or even branchy. Of course once having begun to create plant sculptures the opportunities to experiment with different materials and different shapes are never-ending and I am constantly on the look out for new ideas and inspiration. From sculptures made from the full range of dried flowers and a rich choice of foliages it was a small step to moss, and from moss to wood and shells. Now I feel that there is nothing in the natural world that I cannot use and even go beyond it in pursuit of the original and the new. The pattern I work to changes the whole time. The other day I suddenly got bored of looking at sculptures with single stems and so decided to experiment with multi-stems. I cut lengths of red and green dogwood (cornus) and grouped them together vertically, It created the illusion that the flowers on top were growing directly from them; the effect was startlingly modern and now I shall develop this idea further.

The simplest sculptures to make are the spherical ones: create a round shape out of chicken wire, set it on a base of a length of birch and fill out the wire mesh with your chosen material by inserting the stems into it, whether in bunches or singly, taking care to compact them as closely as possible so the result is a close-textured matt surface. Materials without stems, like moss, should be made more secure with florist's wire, bent like a hairpin and inserted in much the same way. You can vary the height and diameter of the trunk and the size of the sphere as the need dictates. Make sure the base is firmly anchored in your chosen container before beginning as otherwise the sculptures can become top-heavy. Terracotta pots, antique urns and other stoneware are ideal for the purpose as their soft neutral colours tend to complement, rather than detract from or compete with, the decoration. As with all decorations it is the whole that makes the sculpture and the parts should not be conceived in isolation from each other or perceived as such.

LEFT Woodland and the sea-shore are both excellent sources of material for a wide range of decorations. Here there is moss, twisted branches, knotted ivy, white and grey pebbles and beautifully smooth driftwood, all collected by a supplier, John Spikes, who lives in Wales.

ABOVE In this decoration pot-grown amaryllis (or *hippeastrum* as the flower should properly be called) have been set in a shallow straight-sided glass bowl and the bulbs protected by small, rounded, pebbles. The treatment is simple and the result devastating; this easily achieved decoration would lend grace and elegance to any room.

I have always been inspired by the sea and the seashore and love the rough Irish coast as much as the more exotic palm-fringed beaches of the tropics. I find shells an exciting medium to work with: their quality of association is so strong that on sight of a shell I immediately think of the sea. They are particularly suitable for creating still lifes (as in the bathroom in my home) and the enormous range of size and shape, and the appealing variety of colour and texture they offer make shell collages especially fun and rewarding to make. Shells also combine well with other seashore products like dried seaweed, driftwood, sand and smooth rounded pebbles. Such decorations go best in a seaside house, pool area or bathroom, but can be used anywhere as a potent evocation of another world.

Even the city dweller has sufficient access to a wide range of raw materials from which to create a successful decoration. The art is to train the eye to recognize a suitable material and to open the mind to the perpetual stimulus of ideas that nature provides. I have never stopped looking, watching and discovering, and if you do likewise you will begin to appreciate and to be able to use the vast store that this earth has to offer.

LEFT This imposing sculpture is strongly reminiscent of the sea. The frail, pale pink, coral has been placed so it appears to be waving naturally in the water. The creamy coral, shells and sponges adhere together like limpets clutching a rock, the driftwood apparently caught up in it, unable to escape. The green of the plant, designed to appear self-seeded in a crevice, draws the eye as it thrives against all the odds.

RIGHT Shells and corals can also be used effectively to create a spectacular drop, designed to hang inside or outside the house. Surprisingly flexible on a wire base, these drops are extremely heavy and need to be securely anchored at the top. If your furniture and furnishings can be protected, the drops look particularly good just after being sprayed with water.

OVERLEAF These 'trophy' sculptures symbolize man's relationship with his environment – farm and farmer, garden and gardener – and how he strives to control and to use it. Undecorated, the tools look austere and rugged, while the addition of a harvest of dried or fresh flowers, fruits or vegetables softens and romanticizes the image.

DECORATING
THE HOME

The clean lines, flag-stone floor and plain-coloured walls are totally in keeping with this Elizabethan manor house, just re-decorated by David Milinaric. This alcove halfway up the stairs breaks up the otherwise unrelieved expanse of creamy yellow paint; the lavender decoration within it has been shaped like a guardsman's busby, the curved lines at the base echoing the shoulder line of the Chinese pot. At the bottom of the elegant staircase, a magnificent display of dried flowers explodes from a rustic, sculpted pedestal, brightening up the entrance hall. The composition is reminiscent of a Dutch painting; varying coloured hydrangea heads give way to groups of peonies, zinnias, roses, achillea, larkspur and physalis, the overall effect as riotous as any herbaceous border.

A house should be lived in, not a show-case and the most successful interior designers are those that achieve this. I greatly admired the work of John Fowler and David Milinaric, but for me, although she is now retired, that of Nancy Lancaster stands out from all the others. She has a beautiful garden and a passion for flowers and once, during a party she was giving for me, she boomed out, 'Sit down, you're spoiling my room!' Her rooms were sublimely elegant, her taste exquisite, and above all her work was stylish. Her rooms would look grand without being intimidating, a quality surprisingly difficult to achieve. If you entered one of her rooms, you would be stunned and think, this is wonderful'; and success in design is where the style is palpable but at the same time effortless, unselfconscious and without strain. It is crucial to remember that a room that is untouchable, a sofa too perfect to sit on, a dining room too grand for an enjoyable dinner party lack the spark, vitality and warmth essential to my definition of what constitutes a real home.

The most important thing to remember when decorating the home is that a decoration is only an element in a whole scheme, and while it should of course work in its own right, it should be seen and considered in the context in which it is to belong. You would not choose curtain fabric without thinking about the treatment of the walls or floor (or vice versa), neither should you incorporate a sculpture or floral decoration into a room without thinking through its 'fit' or suitability.

Very different moods can be created by the use of different decorations in the same location. TOP The modern multi-stemmed decoration employs black crows' feathers contrasted with russet orange protaea flowers to create a stark, almost sinister effect. The shells, grasses and poppy heads remind me of a collection made on a walk as a child.

CENTRE This decoration is softer than the one above yet still modern. The grasping, bleached, branches of driftwood and looped birch twigs creating a swirl of movement around the peonies (which introduce some necessary colour), the gorse and feathery grasses.

BOTTOM This basket of mixed herbaceous flowers and grasses is much more traditional in mood. The deep red trailing amaranthus provides an escape route from the basket and contrasted with the blue of the larkspur is very striking. Peonies, valerian, heather and roses complete the picture, the composition very much as a fresh decoration using the same materials would have been.

RIGHT This colourful, quirky sculpture would look well in a rustic dining-room or hallway and would complement old oak furniture particularly well. The heavy cracked glaze of the base allows the deep pink of the heather to make maximum impact, while the broken terracotta, bleached wood, moss and prehistoric-looking stones are reminiscent of its natural habitat.

This hallway is long and narrow although the width has been increased by the full-length mirrors. The client's modern chic decoration demanded something slightly unconventional and it seemed appropriate to try to shorten the room by placing this pair of sculptures either end of the twin pedestal hall table. The long stems are firmly anchored in barrel tubs, the heads created from birch twigs bound securely ends down from the top of the trunk and folded back upon themselves.

RIGHT This decoration is situated on a half-landing between a pair of elegantly draped sash windows and immediately catches the eye of anyone on the stairs. Birch is colourful, the attractive reddish-brown lending interest even to a simple decoration, and here picking up the reddish tones in the drapes. The basket holding the decoration, combined with the stone base, moss and birch, creates a pleasing contrast of textures. The lateral birch binding both prevents the other twigs from spreading too far sideways and gives the decoration breadth.

In creating a decoration for a known space the problems that crop up tend to recur. Clients have always sought a solution to the problem of what to put in awkward spaces, dull, dark corners where nothing would grow. Fresh flowers that require re-doing at least once a week are ever an option, but an unsatisfactory one. At first indirectly and tentatively, then explicitly, clients have responded to the development of the use of drieds and sculpture, recognizing their versatility, individuality and attractiveness, and many are now able to give a fairly detailed brief as to what they want, to fit in with the style of their homes.

One's first impression of a house is shaped by the entrance and the hall. But while an unprepossessing exterior can be forgotten, the memory of a hall is rarely erased so readily and its ambience subconsciously flavours all that follows. Frequently gloomy and often lit indirectly or only by artificial light, halls tend to occupy either large, open spaces or small, cramped, narrow ones. In a large space there is the constant danger that a decoration will be 'lost' and in a small space of it being either overwhelming or insignificant. Likewise stair walls pose a problem as they tend to be bleak. As in my own house mirrors can be used to tremendous effect, but make sure you make the most of the available features too. Don't waste the opportunities presented by alcoves, shelves or window ledges. If there are none already it is definitely worth considering installing something: a shelf is easiest and can be sited out of the way, but be careful to locate it in the line of vision as you mount or descend the stairs. In a larger hall a piece of furniture at the foot of or even under the stairs is a practical vehicle for introducing a splash of colour or intrigue; alternatively the same space could be used to house a substantial plant sculpture.

LIVING ROOMS

Time is of the essence in successful decorating – generosity with it, not meanness. While instinct can and should play an important part, a hasty decision is not likely to be a wise one; thought, care, consideration and careful planning are crucial. In addition to the time spent developing an idea and gathering the necessary materials, time is also required for execution. The instant dinner party decoration, created by putting a few potted up plants or fruit and vegetables on the table, is of course quickly achieved, but anything more elaborate, particularly if conceived of as a permanent feature, demands concentration, possibly many hours of labour and, most important, an open mind. A willingness to experiment, a desire constantly to improve what you are doing, a large measure of self-criticism, a striving after perfection are all essential ingredients. I perceive each decoration and every job as an expression of myself and, if I'm not one hundred per cent happy with it, I consider I have sold myself short. If you set yourself the same high standard success will be nearer your grasp.

I was asked to provide some garlands for the fireplace in this stunning drawing room some ten years ago. The glorious, deeply coloured and beautifully carved, old pine panelling immediately made me think of the superb craftsman Grinling Gibbons and I determined to create something in his style. The richly textured, but slightly muted colour palette of dried flowers was perfect for the job, so I set about creating these two drops with artichokes, hydrangea heads, peonies, wheat, nuts, lavender, poppy and thistle heads, and many more – a harvest cornucopia of nature's best. The colours have now faded a little, but the effect is one of maturing and 'antiquing' as the tapestry of colours blends more closely into the background. This decoration proves beyond a shadow of doubt that dried flowers can and will last.

Stylish and gracious living is one of the few common denominators among my clients, whose demands are frequently as challenging as their requirements are individual. My greatest horror is of someone becoming a 'floral victim' by ordering or buying something totally wrong, that is, something that isn't 'them' at all. Fortunately it doesn't happen very often and my regular clients rarely inflict it on me. Halls and living rooms are the easiest areas in a house in which to incorporate a permanent or semi-permanent (designed to last several months) floral decoration because unless you are the sort of person who constantly changes things around the main decorative elements tend to be fixed. Sculptures, still lifes and drieds in majestic urns, with the mood and tonal qualities adjusted to suit the room, can look stunning and take the result far beyond the ordinary. Even rooms which are already extremely stylish can be rounded off by the imaginative use of a floral decoration. A fireplace, for example, a feature which tends to draw the eye wherever and whenever it is situated in a room can be used to create a particularly magnificent effect, and whereas fresh flowers react badly to the heat when the fire's lit, the draught when it's not, and worst of all to changes of temperature, drieds are quite happy in a changeable environment as, of course, are sculptures employing metal and stone.

ABOVE This attractive, dusky yellow, topiary-shaped sculpture set in a mahogany urn would brighten up any dull corner. The head has been made from the curry plant (*Helichrysum augustifolium*), a half-hardy perennial shrub which carries small clusters of flowers from June to August. With its silvery grey foliage it makes a hard-working member of a border and is easy to dry (hung upside down in bunches). Variations on this sculpture can be made by creating a mushroom shape, using a coloured flower head for the rounded top edge, and something contrasting, like silvery grey artemisia, or lamb's tongue (*stachys*), lichen or moss for the underside, to represent the gills.

RIGHT My brief for this commission was to use my imagination as to what I felt would be appropriate for the client. The house is full of successful contrasts between very modern and very old things. I decided that it would be best to create something abstract and came up with this sculpture (in fact there are two). The layers of tortured barbed wire clinging to the closely grouped birch stems (which make up the trunk) culminate in a giant ball. This is alive with a fascinating swirl of movement and has a deeply contoured texture created by the black holes between the twists of wire. The vertical grooves of the metal dustbin at the base send the eye naturally upwards to the main sphere of interest.

This trophy sculpture is one of a pair either side of French windows leading out to a small patio garden. I had been playing with the idea of coupling a trophy sculpture with a mirror for some time and this client presented me with the opportunity to experiment. The chocolate brown walls had already established a mysterious, intriguing atmosphere which is heightened by the reflective pools of the mirrors and their rustic, terracotta-painted surrounds. The dried lavender, apparently growing from the pot, brings the sculpture alive, while the row of smaller terracotta pots at the base, carrying chunky, scented candles nestling in moss, appear like votive offerings lighting up a shrine and add to the air of mystery.

More often than not style goes hand in hand with individualism; the thought of creating something original excites me and many of my commissions have been executed in response to a unique demand or situation. Sometimes this gives me an opportunity to develop an idea that I have had some time before but not had a chance to explore fully. Some ideas remain dormant for a long time, years even; some a faint glimmer that need to be teased out; some already partially thought through some the beginnings of something much greater, perhaps a totally new concept in decorating, introducing an extra dimension that will eventually percolate through the business and become a standard feature: that is the joy of ideas and at the root of my love affair with nature – you never know where they will lead you until you realize you have arrived. Sometimes I become consciously aware that what I am doing is only an interim measure – necessary and no less satisfying for all that – but nevertheless only a staging post. At the moment, for instance, I know that there is a vast amount of unexplored potential in the use of mirrors in decoration and I find the challenge that that knowledge presents acts as a constant stimulus.

Sofas, chairs, lamps, ornaments and any other sort of decoration often look better in pairs. Apart from the simple fact that if you want something to be noticed you stand a better chance of success with two, pairs are definitely more stylish. They are also more formal and implicitly suggest to the onlooker that here you have a scheme that has been put together with some thought and care – which of course is true. Sometimes it is not practical – either because a pair can't be found or for reasons of space – but with floral decorations creating two instead of one is rarely a problem and I am frequently called on to do this by clients, both at my instigation and theirs.

One of the key things to remember when decorating a room is to maintain a balance; internally within each decorative element, but also overall. In floral terms it is important to make sure you include a mixture of decorative types and styles of decoration – a sculpture, a fresh decoration, a dried decoration and some pot pourri – nothing but dried flowers in a room is as potentially boring as a garden full of conifers; the drieds should be alleviated by a bowl of fresh flowers: roses, spring bulbs, wild flowers or whatever is in season. Likewise remember that a plant sculpture is fulfilling the same role as a piece of furniture or an ornament and so, on occasion, an additional decoration in that room will be appropriate. Be careful also to vary the shapes of your decorations and to ensure that the shape suits the designated location: if, for instance, you make all the decorations in a room conical or all of them spherical, they won't look smart but just silly, however admirable the individual pieces may be. Apart from the room itself, the 'container' I am asked to use by a client may play a vital part in establishing what sort of decoration will result. This may sound obvious, but if you imagine the huge range of possibilities encompassed by a laundry basket, a terracotta urn, an antique cradle and a goldfish bowl the seemingly infinite choice begins to become apparent.

ABOVE Back in the Elizabethan manor house, this upstairs room is used as a playroom. With its nursery connotations, this now redundant, handsomely carved, antique cradle is an ideal vehicle for a decoration. Devastating in its simplicity, it has been filled only with a mass of corn on the turn, the full ears of wheat suggestive of the abundance of nature and the eternal cycle of rebirth and renewal.

RIGHT White flowers, especially lilies, inspire in me a great feeling of peace and tranquillity. They look beautiful and arresting wherever you put them, but look particularly well in a garden room set against white wrought iron furniture and a backdrop of other greenery. Here, in the foreground, white lilies have been planted into a rustic wicker basket, finished off with a large raffia bow; at the back, more lilies are displayed with cow's parsley in a basket painted white; next to them, on a small table, a white begonia has been planted in a moss-lined goldfish bowl to create a smooth well-rounded, full effect; adjacent to the lilies on the bench, thrusting,

budding amaryllis have been combined with bare, bleached branches and bound with raffia in a moss encrusted pot, poised to burst open into their full glory.

OVERLEAF This pair of lavender topiary sculptures looks magnificent in this stylish, mutely coloured drawing room. Their soft hazy mauve hue perfectly complements the sponged walls, antique mirror and books and adds to the relaxing atmosphere of the sitting area. The thick plaited raffia trim at the top of the urns creates an interesting contrast in texture.

KITCHENS AND DINING ROOMS

As with a bathroom 'decorating' a kitchen is not generally thought to be necessary, although of course the units, tiles and colour scheme will probably have been thought through. Because of this, almost anything you do by way of decoration will attract attention and can also usefully serve to distract from ugly gadgets and the merely functional. Kitchen decorations should above all be fun. They should entertain or amuse the onlooker whether your kitchen is stream-lined hi-tech, purely functional or countrified, and as far from the conventional as possible.

The most obvious materials to use for kitchen decorations are those associated with food and cooking. Dried herbs are decorative and practical, as when fresh are not available you can, of course, use them. Bunches of herbs can be ranged along the top of units filling the gap between them and the ceiling in a room where a few inches' gap allows this (as in mine). Herbs can also be hung in bunches, either against the wall, or directly from the ceiling, but don't forget to tighten the binding if you use them regularly or they'll end up all over the floor (and drieds don't wash well!). Herbs also look well growing in pots and can be made into a feature if displayed attractively. Some, like parsley, I use so often that I prefer to have it in the kitchen rather than outside anyway. As it is used more for its decorative effect than taste, it is all too easy to forget to pick it if you grow it outside.

Apart from using herbs for decoration, you can create an attractive still life with fruit and vegetables – some, like chillies, peppers, artichokes and mushrooms dry well if you want a more permanent feature. Any surface can be used for a still life but if your work surfaces are precious to you and you have either no kitchen table or a very

Baskets of bread work well as decorations in a kitchen and are fun both to have and to make. ABOVE The decoration has been kept fairly simple combining wheat, poppy heads, French sticks, and glazed shaped rolls covered in poppy seeds in a traditional bread basket which has been given additional twisted handles for added interest. The rough hessian bow gives the piece a finished air.

RIGHT This decoration is a far more complex sculpture, designed especially to go on top of these chevron patterned kitchen units. Similar materials – wheat, poppy heads, loaves of bread and rolls, and a wicker basket – with the addition of honesty, dried cow's parsley, grasses and a substantial terracotta storage jar have been arranged on a moss base into a still life, the basket carefully placed so that it looks as though it has just been dropped.

small one, you may find plenty of space on top of the refrigerator, on top of the upper units, or even on a specially erected shelf. Decorative swags on the wall are also effective.

Rustic baskets are particularly good as the base of a display as they are closely associated in the imagination with produce, and the good, healthy and desirable things in life. Wooden or terracotta bowls conjure up similar images.

Other materials ideal for making decorations for a kitchen are all those associated with baking. You could make a still-life sculpture in the 'trophy' style with wooden spoons, a rolling pin, whisk and meat mallet, perhaps filled out with corn or rye grass. Bunches of golden corn tied with raffia look very attractive and for a simple effect you could display it by itself, or, for something more complex, grouped into a still life with bread in a basket.

Do be careful if you decide to use bread in a still life though as it can attract mice, and you must coat the loaves with polyurethane to stop them going mouldy. One day I got a furious call from a restaurant to whom we had supplied a pair of trophies of garden tools and bread (which we would go in to tidy up from time to time) to say that a family of mice were nesting in a cottage loaf and would we kindly remove them. Apparently the worst possible had happened and a baby mouse had dropped down into a client's soup! I couldn't help laughing, but it taught me always to be on the look out, although I like to think that in a modern building one is fairly safe.

Table decorations can be made to all shapes and sizes and vary in their complexity. Sometimes the occasion – perhaps an informal supper or lunch – demands only something simple and you could make one along the lines of one of these shown here. FAR RIGHT A combination of walnuts, polished chestnuts and pecan nuts has been stuck onto a wire base set in a closely woven basket to create a deceptively straightforward decoration, very autumnal in feel. TOP Almost more readily than anything else candles establish a festive, celebratory mood. Combined with fresh flowers in this formally based, springlike decoration the effect is very romantic and appealing. The flowers I have used are camellias, lilies of the valley, pinks, grape hyacinths and winter-flowering jasmine. BOTTOM This cheerful, summery decoration has been made from a mixed group of ranunculus planted in an open, shallow basket. The moss at the base, allowed to escape through a (deliberate) tear in the basket gives a natural effect.

In some ways decorations designed to accompany food are more difficult to do than any other but they are also an excellent vehicle for experiment. On the one hand they need to be more than just stylish: they need to be immediately alluring and to stimulate all the senses, especially the appetite; while on the other, because they are by nature usually temporary, one can afford to be more daring, more ambitious and more quixotic. More permanent decorations in dining-rooms need not, and probably should not, try to achieve so much, Just as in any other room, a large decoration will be perceived as part of the furniture and therefore should merely complement the rest of the room and the furniture and furnishings in it.

If you enjoy and frequently do give elaborate dinner or lunch parties where the table decorations play a large part in setting the tone of the occasion, then even more should you beware of dressing up other parts of the room: the most splendid piece of confectionery, set on the sideboard for your guests to drool over in anticipation during the rest of the meal, could all too easily be overwhelmed or diminished by a dramatic display of fresh flowers placed too near it. Decide what is most important to you about an occasion: if you know the food will be excellent and well-presented, don't detract from it by attempting something over-elaborate with your decorations or make sure you place them judiciously; if you are wor-

ried about the food (or it is not important to you) you can and should make more of a show with the decorations, allowing them to be more dramatic, and to make a statement about your party. And if, at one extreme, you have a prize camellia in a pot that you would like all your friends to admire, it is perfectly legitimate to set it in the middle of the dining-table and serve a very simple meal. None of them will leave without commenting on it. Nevertheless, you should really aim to achieve a balance between decorations and food as *both* are part of the occasion but, as I have already pointed out, whatever degree of prominence you want your table decorations to have, no occasion should be celebrated without them.

FAR RIGHT This client has a tremendous sense of style which is evident all over her house. About three years ago she asked me to provide her with something to go in the alcoves on either side of the superb, open fireplace in the dining room. She didn't want plants as it was too dark for them and the care of them would be too time-consuming, so I came up with an idea for a pair of birch sculptures. The simple forest of graceful twigs, rising phoenix-like from a graceful antique urn, relates beautifully with the rich, faded, rustic style of the room and requires nothing but the occasional dust.

RIGHT The formality of this table setting is belied by the rustic simplicity of the candlesticks, made from small terracotta pots. The centrepiece is made up of a glorious display of pink flowers – extravagant lilies, roses and gerbera. The green, ivy-patterned tablecloth is made from one of my own range of fabrics.

Lighting, the relationship of the table to the rest of the room, the decorations on the table itself, are all important in establishing the right mood for a party. BELOW AND RIGHT The tall antique candelabra are balanced by the low squat artichokes which are playing host to nightlights in heat-treated glasses. The centrepiece itself is a jungley display of green bananas and red roses, held in check by the strong verticals of the sugar cane, tied with raffia.

This decoration is surprisingly complex in its make-up. A basket contains an eclectic mix of flowers and plants: artichokes on a bed of banana leaves and parsley crowd round pots of thyme, while pink hydrangea heads compete with miniature red roses for dominance on the handle. Note how the greens of the foliage merge with the ivy tablecloth and the reds of the napkins match that of the roses, giving an impression of unity.

Think of the whole table and plan the decoration as part of it, not as an adjunct to it. The colour scheme needs to be thought through: there will be choices to be made of linen, china, candles as well as the flowers, and they all have to work together. Depending on the size of the table you might like to give each guest their own decoration instead of, or as well as, a centre-piece. The candlesticks should be made to work too; if you don't have anything suitable or want a change from your usual ones try making your own using an egg-cup, moss and raffia, adding hessian or ivy for variety, or scooping the hearts from globe artichokes and using them instead. Anything that appears to be an individual touch, something new and original will always flatter the guests. A crisp white napkin, rolled and tied with ivy, a sprig of herbs or a posy tucked in the folds, a cabbage or vine leaf used as a table mat, a shiny magnolia leaf as a place card, all suggest that thought has gone into giving your guests pleasure and will be much appreciated.

If you don't want to use flowers at all, why not use fruit and vegetables, which can work as well as, if not better than, flowers. But whatever decorations you use to enliven your dinner parties remember that what matters most is that you please yourself.

THE ART OF
SPECIAL
OCCASIONS

CHRISTMAS

Decorations for special occasions are particularly fun to do as they are naturally celebratory. Christmas, birthdays, anniversaries, weddings, barmitzvahs, feast days all provide an excellent opportunity and excuse (should it be needed) to do something out of the ordinary, something special. More than any other these sort of decorations need to be thought of as part of a scheme, not in isolation from each other, as there are likely to be many individual pieces involved and several different elements. These should all be linked by a well thought out theme, so that the decorations at once appear to be part of a coherent concept and not just put together any-old-how.

The occasion itself will often inspire the idea for a theme and this is particularly true of a seasonal feast like Christmas or Thanksgiving. Christmas was a very happy and magical time for me as a child and those memories are very important to me. There was no question of buying a tree: I was the one who would have to go out to the woods near the house, choose the tree, cut it down and bring it home. Even then the glittery side of Christmas never really appealed to me, and the gloss and baubles available commercially simply do not sum up what Christmas is all about. For me it is an occasion that should take us back to our roots, cause us to consider why we are here and think of our relationship with the earth that feeds us, an occasion to reflect on the quintessential things in life. It is also of course, a feast, and a gathering, an extension of the harvest and of Thanks-

giving, and an opportunity to rejoice in the pleasures of good company, good food and a spirit of goodwill.

Christmas decorations should therefore be as natural and as countrified as possible, full of rustic charm – festoons and trails of ivy, branches of holly and larch, mosses, lichen, mistletoe, fir cones, fruits and nuts. More natural decorations are now coming back into fashion and rustic-style decorations made from wood, cinnamon sticks and old-fashioned pomanders can be found in the shops if you don't want to make all of your own.

This Christmas table created for a client sums up rustic chic. The room and the furnishings are all extremely elegant, and the decorations succeed in introducing a rustic, natural note without destroying this because the colours and textures have been chosen to complement it. The theme I have adopted is of sleds, specially crafted in wicker, which run the length of the table, laden not with gift-wrapped parcels but forest fruits. Holly, fir cones, mistletoe, lichen encrusted twigs, larch and fruit and nuts jostle for space in them and large

tartan bows (made from fabric not ribbon) have been tied to the ends of the sleds and contribute to the festive air. Between and at each end of the sleds, baskets filled with fir, fruit, nuts and bundles of cinnamon sticks hold candles in pockets of wicker round the sides. More candles give light from small terracotta pots and saucers and the scent from these combined with the heady smells from the fir, cinnamon sticks and blazing fire conjure up pleasing images of the forest, with a hint of the exotic.

The spaces on either side of this extravagantly draped window are ideal for a striking pair of decorations. Based on the idea of the traditional pedestal, they succeed in achieving something far less conventional and far more interesting. At the heart of each display is a large salmon-pink poinsettia, whose clearly visible terracotta pot gives it a rustic look. Above and behind branches of larch, spruce and birch reach for the ceiling, fleshed out with red-berried holly and yellow-flowered mahonia. The poinsettia itself appears to be sprouting variegated holly, which partially veils the magnificent moss bow, whose 'ribbons' reach right down to the floor, disguising the stem of the pedestal. Between the twin decorations a moss basket, tied at one end of the handle with raffia and holding some shiny red apples, sits on the elegant table in front of the window.

The decorations should make the house homely and welcoming, warm and inviting and they should be fun, lively and amusing as well as attractive. If you have an open fireplace, a roaring fire always creates a convivial atmosphere and the mantelshelf makes an excellent focal point for the decorations in the room as people are naturally drawn towards the fire. Candles shed a soft warm glow that even lights with dimmers can never match, and you should use them liberally in and among your decorations. I am always teased about the lights I use on my Christmas tree: they are designed to look like candles so I painstakingly arrange them so that they stand precisely upright, carrying through the charade. Attention to that sort of detail is crucial if your decorations are to be really successful and, although my friends may laugh as they watch me, the results more than justify the trouble taken. Candlesticks and candelabra for real candles, made from suitably rustic materials like terracotta, wicker, moss, hessian and birch (held together with raffia or florists' wire), are unusual, can be fun to make and will contribute to the general air of festivity in your scheme.

Always slow to recognize the value of their assets, it has taken the Americans to show the British the decorative potential of the immensely varied, rich and colourful Irish and Scottish tartans. The cheerful reds and greens are traditional Christmas colours and work particularly well in conjunction with the rustic materials mentioned above. Many styles and widths of ribbon are now available and are extremely useful as swags and tied into bows (as decorations in their own right) and as a finish for more elaborate pieces. Tartan fabric looks effective used as a drape, gathered into a drop, as an additional festive covering for a chair or sofa and even works well used as napkins and tablecloth.

It is much easier to get hold of foliage – mostly evergreen – and berries at Christmas time as they are in season then, and once you begin to differentiate between the many different evergreens the range is quite startling: it included ivies, hollies, box, many different conifers (for instance pine, spruce and juniper), berberis and mahonia. But as well as these there are a few fresh flowers traditionally used for decoration at this time of year. Poinsettias (*Euphorbia pulcherrima*) are the splashiest of these; generally grown as pot plants, it is in fact the bracts of the flowers rather than the flowers themselves which are the prime source of attraction: elliptical in shape, they come in colours ranging from deep crimson, through scarlet and soft pink, to a greenish white. Pushed up in price by the festive season, it is often cheaper to buy several smaller ones than one large, and either group them together or repot them in a large container, disguising the base with moss. Water only sparingly. Another flower in season at this time is *Helleborus niger* (the Christmas rose); they are ideal potted in a small basket or fresh-picked in a table decoration. The flowers last a reasonable length of time as long as they are kept well-watered and are not subjected to extremes of temperature. Winter jasmine, *Viburnum fragrans* and winter flowering cherry are also likely to be out at this time if the winter has been a mild one.

This drop, one of a pair, hangs at the entrance to a drawing room and represents my idea of Christmas. Many houses have sconces on the walls for candles and lights so it occurred to me that it would be fun and original to make some; and, not only would they look attractive, they would also bring life and light to a dreary corner. Candlelight fascinates wherever it is and however it is used, and the effect here of its shadows playing on the contrasting textures of the rustic materials and the flock wallpaper is devastating.

LEFT I set up this Christmas table for Thomas Goode, the fine china and glass shop in South Audley Street, London and, again, despite the splendour of the surroundings the rustic style works very well. The attention to detail is the important thing: note the spruce garlands hanging from the ceiling and the tartan bows at the corners of the table as well as on the chair backs. As the table is not very large I wanted to keep it relatively free of decoration so as not to clutter it, so I thought it would be fun to decorate the backs of the chairs instead. Small Christmas trees have been set into pockets made of a tough green fabric, which were then tied to the backs of the chairs. The tartan bows are decorative rather than functional. On the table itself I decided to make a feature of the candelabra; I constructed these from birch poles set in terracotta pots and lashed them together with a thin rope. A small rustic centrepiece, also designed to hold candles, together with small parcels of moss tied with tartan ribbon, complete the picture.

BELOW A decorative wreath on the front door at Christmas at once establishes a festive mood. Here the thick base has been made from fir, which has then been overlaid with a smaller circlet of variegated holly, a selection of fruit, nuts, wheat and gilded pine cones. A multi-looped bow at the top of the wreath completes the effect. Each item is held together and fixed to the base with florists' wire.

ABOVE The grand setting (the Victoria and Albert Museum) for this decoration seemed to demand an element of glitter among the rustic materials which the bright gold of the winged cherub provides. The bright red dogwood bows and baskets of red and yellow apples contribute to the particularly flamboyant style of this drop. The decoration shows quite clearly how important the grouping of materials is in creating a strong statement. The spindly larch twigs spattered with fir cones relieve the strong linear thrust of the decoration and give the display breadth.

If you find the rustic style not quite extravagant enough, you can of course always introduce some gold, some silver and some glitter into your decorations to make them more so, while the setting you plan for them might dictate this anyway. Any of the rustic forest materials, other foliage and fruits and vegetables can be sprayed or painted with metallic paint to give a solid or a distressed effect, as can baskets, pots and any other props. Bare deciduous branches also spray well and their elegant sweeps can look supremely graceful used as just one element within a decoration or alone, perhaps in an urn finished at the base with a bow. An impression of grandeur can be created with elaborate swags and garlands made from pliable foliage like ivy, moss and lengths of fabric and these can be decorated further with bows or rosettes. Bows are particularly useful in creating a festive note whether tied onto gift-wrapped parcels or above pictures, used as punctuation on a swag or as a footnote to a much larger decoration.

The rich gold of this decoration has been simply achieved by spraying the raw materials with gold lacquer paint. A more subtle effect could be achieved by antiquing or 'distressing' them instead. The drop comprises palm fronds, bramble leaves, bracken (fern), wheat, fungi, poppy heads, walnuts, apples and peppers.

123

These decorations are part of a series done for the night-club Annabels. The idea was to transform the whole building into a romantic, fairy-tale style castle, with the alcoves in the rooms made to look like windows, with views out from the castle over a wooded, snow-covered, landscape. We thought it would be fun to have dogs looking longingly in through the window, to see what was going on. The entrance was made to look like a hunting lodge with a rustic bar, which then led on into the castle.

PARTIES

Parties for weddings, birthdays, barmitzvahs, anniversaries and other special occasions should first and foremost be designed to give pleasure and enjoyment, both to the host and to the guests. If it does not, the party has failed, and you should remember this when you are planning the decorations. A party where the decorations are noticeably sparse, where the scheme has gone awry or where the decorations are too vulgar has fallen at the first hurdle, which is to create an aura of excitement and vitality into which the guests are swept the moment they arrive. If, on the other hand, the decorations are spectacular and the mood they establish is a happy and inspiring one, the party stands a much better chance of being a success. Smell is also important in achieving this and you should incorporate a means of producing a pleasant one into your scheme, whether through candles, pot pourri or flowers.

As I said earlier, it is important to have a theme to work to, and you should decide on this early on in your planning so you have time to elaborate and develop it. The theme could be based on something as simple as a colour or a type of flower; it could be a mood – romantic for a girl's coming of age, mysterious for Hallowe'en; a period – the Middle Ages, the eighteenth century, the 1920s, the 1960s; or it could be a form of stage set transporting the guests to another world – the seaside, a ship, a garden, the tropics, a fairground. The essential thing is to be consistent about it even if you don't want to make it all-embracing – with costumes, food and drink and music to fit. If you're working to a particular colour scheme, make sure the flowers, the marquee, the waiters' shirts and your own outfit at least don't clash with it and at best complement or conform to it. A bride with a pink and white bouquet in a yellow and white striped marquee will not look her best.

ABOVE The focal point of this exuberant decoration is the large basket overflowing with lemons, which has been 'antiqued' with silver paint. The lush, exotic nature of the lemons has been picked up by the tall stems of the tuber roses, while the rustic note struck by the basket is carried through by the use of fern, cow's parsley and moss. Note how this decoration is making good use of available space: in this instance the top of a boxed-in radiator.

RIGHT Suitable as a centrepiece for a small round table, this decoration has been made using a single colour – white – contrasted with the green of the foliage and is effective in its simplicity. I have used camellias, freesias (as much for their scent as their beauty), daisies, lily of the valley, dianthus, Christmas rose and apple blossom.

FAR RIGHT This rich, rustic, yet elegant, decoration was made in the 'trophy' style as part of a yellow and white scheme for a birthday celebration. Daffodils combine with lilies, syringa, cow's parsley, forsythia, eucalyptus and bunches of grapes to fill out the white-painted tools which appear slightly weathered, deliberately touched with green.

These three photographs show elements of a scheme of decorations
I created for a formal reception and dinner at Osterley Park, a beautiful,
originally Elizabethan house, completely remodelled by Adam in
the second half of the eighteenth century. The outstanding plasterwork,
handsome pictures and fine proportions of the rooms must all be
complemented by the decorations which should work with the existing
features rather than seeking to outdo them in magnificence.
Pink and white was chosen as the theme especially to enhance the
indigenous colour scheme. Large double roses, lilies, orchids, tropical
palmate leaves and thick-stemmed candles contribute to
an overall effect of rich elegance.

The range of decorations you can produce for a party and the degree of attention to detail you can go into is limitless, but each decoration must serve a purpose. If the party is to be held in a small space, for instance, the most effective way of decorating the room might well be to dress the walls and the light fittings (not forgetting the cables), and to make the most of the corners which, unless they have either a decoration or a piece of furniture in them, often represent wasted space. If you are having food, and therefore tables, you will usually find some space for a decoration on them, even if it is only a small one, and you may find that the decorations will be most effective if you concentrate on just one area – such as the tables. In marquees and large rooms, pillars and poles positively beg to be decorated and should not be left unadorned without very good reason.

Do make the most of features already in a room, although you should also be prepared to put in some of your own to create a special effect – whether urns, statues or trees. Sometimes the setting for a party, whether it is in hired premises or your own home, creates as many problems as opportunities. The native decoration, especially when it is well done and the rooms are impressive in size and quality of decorative detail, may well effectively limit the decorative treatment you give, unless you are planning a wholesale transformation and complete disguise. Large pictures (perhaps Old Masters), a dominant colour scheme, both mean the decorator must follow where others have led, but wherever possible make a virtue of necessity at the same time. If in such surroundings you succeed in creating a decorative scheme that not only complements the setting but also stands out in it then you have done well indeed.

Permanent features in a room may be able to be turned to advantage and you should always be on the look-out for these. An open doorway presents an unparalleled opportunity for a glimpse of the whole scheme, whose proportions may not be apparent from inside the room itself; mirrors can be used to create unexpected effects with reflections; and alcoves are capable of absorbing large decorations without these becoming too prominent.

Lots of small tables laid out in a large room is the way many people decide to seat a large number of guests for dinner. Apart from making life considerably easier for the staff, this arrangement has the attraction of enabling the guests to imagine themselves, for the course of the meal at least, at a small intimate dinner party, and not at a gathering (however grand) for hundreds, all being served identical food and wines. The challenge for the decorator is to make each of these tables individual, a little bit different from its neighbour, so that each guest is made to feel special and important among the throng. Occasionally the differences I make in the tables are such that only a discerning eye would notice them, done more for my own enjoyment than anyone else's, but none the less a detail that I like to feel has been attended to. In spite of the need to make the tables intimate, guests do like to see each other and you should be careful not to make any larger decorations between the tables too obtrusive although they are useful in varying the pace and for introducing an explosive charge of interest and of colour.

It helps if a large room is constructed on different levels, perhaps with a stage on which all eyes may be made to focus. A variation in level helps the decorator enormously by creating troughs and peaks of interest, and if there are none, I will create some if I possibly can, accentuating the differences between them by making a feature out of the steps that join them.

ABOVE The yellow and white decorations for this formal wedding reception held in the Ballroom at Grosvenor House Hotel, London were chosen to reflect a spring theme. The stage (top left) acted as a focal point and the large decorations between the tables were carefully placed to avoid obscuring the view, both of it and the rest of the room. They are none the less a rich source of attraction, the candles in their midst adding to their resemblance to a shooting, then cascading firework. Note how each of the centrepiece decorations on the tables are quite different but all conform to the same broad theme.

RIGHT This dramatically sited (at the end of a corridor against a dark background) decoration looks as though it could have been brought straight in from the garden, where the urn would have marked the top of a flight of steps or the end of a balustrade. The rich, rounded extravagance of the orchids is beautifully contrasted with the deceptive delicacy of the variegated ivy, growing happily through and below them. The moss, just visible through the fronds, is disguising the container and adds to the surprisingly rustic appeal of the display, otherwise belied by the orchids.

My brief in supplying these decorations for a bar mitzvah in an English country setting was simply to strike a fun note for the occasion. The use of vegetables in decorations, particularly on this scale, is still comparatively unusual and is therefore popular for its novelty value as much as for the interesting and unusual decorative effects it is possible to create with them. Here the marquee had been erected to take in the garden pond and a number of trees and shrubs, giving me the opportunity to capitalize on the water ABOVE Pillar candelabra like this one, using a half-barrel as a base, studded the edge of the dance floor, each one slightly different. I combined groups of rosy red apples, artichokes, cabbages, hydrangea heads, hips, laurel and privet with deep pink roses, all set in a bed of moss, in living, growing pyramids over six feet high.

Sometimes clients have very strong views about what they want from their parties or on certain elements that they would like the decorations to incorporate, no matter what the overall direction is. This happens particularly with marquees that tend to be erected in the client's garden and must either avoid or take in certain prized features. Marquees often pose far greater technical problems than bricks and mortar do – partly because of their flimsy nature and partly because of the peculiar quality of light that the lining inevitably seems to give. Rarely water, more often trees, shrubs and borders can be brought within a marquee presenting me with the bare bones of the decorative structure. Water is a particular bonus as with careful lighting it can be made to work like a mirror, creating interesting reflections, patterns and shadows. Don't automatically exclude as much of the garden as possible from a marquee: think first what advantages certain features might bring and make a properly considered decision, if necessary overcoming a natural inclination towards the conventional.

My innovation of the use of vegetables in decoration has been one of the most significant advances in floral design in the last few years, vastly increasing the range of materials that we are able to offer clients. Constantly experimenting with different materials it suddenly occurred to me that there was a whole area of nature whose products had barely been tapped for their decorative effects. Fruits and vegetables have always been used by artists in still-life painting, so why not in floral decoration? So I proceeded to experiment, at first mixing them in with flowers and more traditional materials, then to use them for less conventional decorations like sculptures. Now they form an integral part of my palette and I would not be without them both for their strong vibrant colours and for their contrasting textures, from the smooth skin of the aubergine (egg plant) to the exquisitely crinkled leaf of a Savoy cabbage. From vegetable products it was a small step to the woodland, the health and the seashore and now any combination of them might provide me with inspiration for a party.

The table decorations for the meal were particularly enjoyable to do as they provided a marked contrast with the formality of the place settings with provision for several courses and as many different wines. With the otherwise monochrome tables, it was important to introduce some colour, which the use of vegetables made easy. RIGHT Pink roses have been married with a large cabbage and ivy on a base of terracotta bounded by a small hand fork, trowel and bamboo canes. The four candlesticks have been made from lengths of birch covered in moss at either end and set in terracotta pots. BELOW In this decoration lengths of wood create a palisade to keep the vegetables in place and to provide a strong vertical line, on this table not established by the candlesticks. The palisade vainly attempts to keep artichokes, chilli peppers, apples and grapes within its bounds, while more artichokes are used as candle-holders.

RIGHT Even the two sides of this decoration could belong to different tables. I have used hessian to create the base of the decoration, suggestive of a sack of vegetables, and again, tied with raffia, to cover the terracotta pots which are used as candlesticks. Beautifully scrubbed carrots cluster with aubergines (egg plant), tomatoes, Savoy cabbage, bunches of parsley and sweet-smelling rosemary, creating a strong display of varied textures and colours.

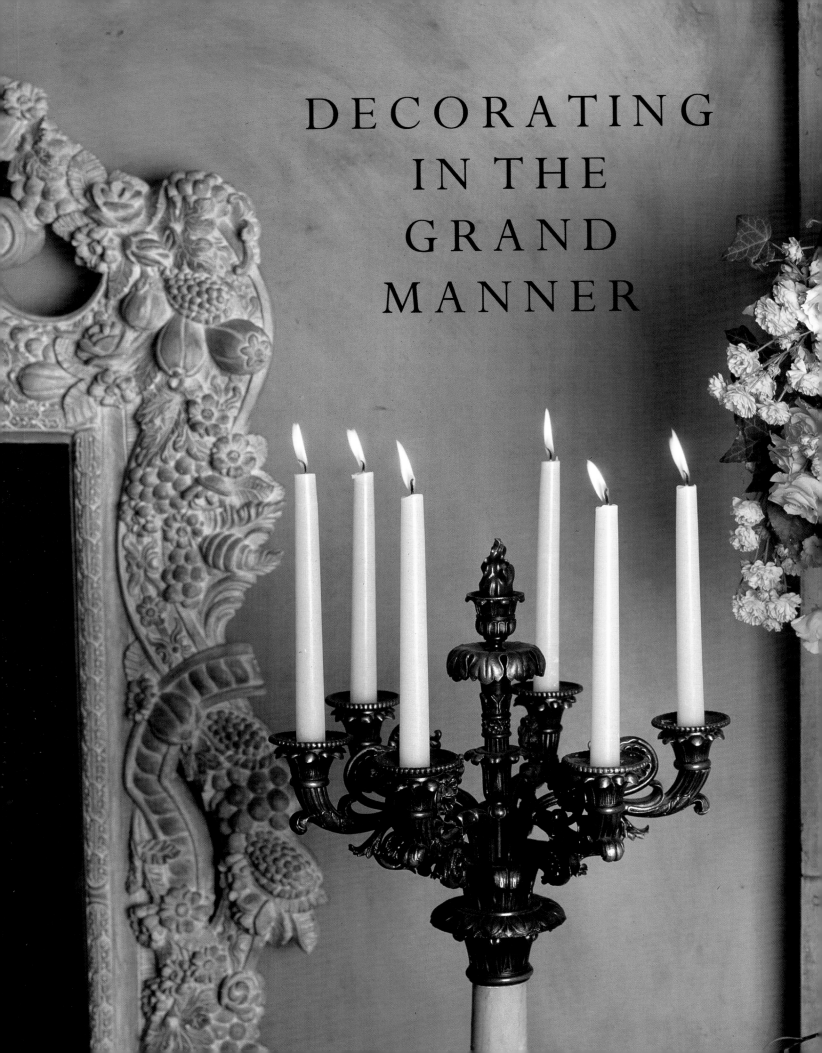

DECORATING
IN THE
GRAND
MANNER

Being asked to set the mood or create a theme for an entire party is the most challenging and the most rewarding of all commissions. These grand affairs often present an opportunity for me to fulfil an artistic fantasy that already exists in my head but that I have not been able to afford to put into effect. More often than not either the client will give me a pointer as to what is required (which will set me off on a train of creative thought) or, if not, the venue itself can play a large part in deciding which direction to go in.

Ideas gather like snowballs on these occasions and usually, although I do consult the client, they rarely have any real conception of what I am planning to do. Those that know me better get more of an inkling, experience enabling them to flesh out the outlines I give, but often experience will also have taught them that it is best to leave me to my own devices.

My problem in doing these spectacular parties is that, whatever the occasion, in my mind it rapidly becomes my own party. I become obsessive about what I want to do, about how the project is developing and perfectionist in its execution so that I and my team frequently finish only as the first guests begin to arrive. The angst for all concerned is considerable, and it is probably fortunate that these events only crop up two or three times a year. But the results do make it all worthwhile. As long as I feel I have genuinely delighted and amazed the client, created something beyond their wildest dreams, then that for me is the moment of fulfilment.

I try to create something original and to explore different themes each time I'm given such a commission, and no two events will ever be exactly alike. Sometimes I'm asked to reproduce something I've done before, and this happens on the small as well as the large scale, but I hate doing it as I feel I should constantly be moving on, not repeating the past. When I first brought full-grown trees into a ballroom – cherry trees in flower – it was a staggering success. The idea was new and exciting, but now it is done so often – by other decorators as much as myself – that I resist doing it, even when asked specifically, favouring something new.

The magnificent setting for this formal dinner is the dining room at Apsley House, No. 1, London, at Hyde Park Corner, remodelled for the Duke of Wellington by the Wyatt brothers in the late 1820s. The extravagant Regency style is here well reflected in the rich red wall fabric and liberal use of gilt in the door and picture frames. The sheer opulence of the decorative treatment meant I would have been foolish to attempt to do anything but complement and enhance it with my own scheme for the dinner table. I therefore chose red relieved with pink as my main colour using double roses to echo the extravagance of the setting. I created a tall centrepiece to correct the proportions of the table in relation to the very high ceiling of the room and made it double as a candelabra. Branch candlesticks decorated with roses and foliage were set at intervals the length of the table, interspersed with baskets of the same flowers. To add to the luxury of the overall impression I then garlanded the backs of the chairs with a thick rope of the same red and pink roses. The magnificence of the scheme is due to its scale, but the same devices could be used in a much smaller way to create a setting of great charm.

A GARDEN IN THE TROPICS

The idea behind this party was to create a set that succeeded in being both tropical and elegant. The hostess was leaving London to live in Paris and wanted to wish her friends *au revoir* in style. The venue she had chosen was Claridges, one of London's finest hotels.

BELOW Dramatic lighting, casting vivid shadows helped enormously in creating the right atmosphere for the party. On this table set for dinner, the towering bamboo is girdled at the base with brightly coloured flowers – lilies, crocosmia – and lush foliage, and the sheer vitality of the decoration belies the formality of the table setting. Twin candles have been wrapped in hessian, giving the base the look of a coconut.

RIGHT A pair of these waterfalls greeted the guests as they entered the party, at once taking them out of the world outside, establishing a tropical mood and setting the tone for the rest of the evening. Autumn foliage has been combined with lush palms, ferns, strelitzia, moss, bamboo, fallen branches and of course the cascading water, to create an idyllic grotto, that might easily be found on a tropical island.

It was a promising beginning for elegance, but the tropicality was more of a problem. We wanted to make the entrance appear to be part of a palace courtyard, on a remote paradise island somewhere in the Pacific, so we had to do something radical: I persuaded Claridges to allow us to take up the carpet from the entrance and the bare floor at once helped to banish the image of a luxury hotel. On each side of the entrance I created a working waterfall, lit the area by myriad candles burning in large pots, and brought in masses and masses of trees to create a jungley effect. Here the guests had drinks and then, for dinner, they were led into the ballroom as though into a magical starlit garden filled with groves of graceful bamboo and birds of paradise (*strelitzia*) which normally I would never dream of using. In fact, my client had specifically forbidden me to use them as she can't stand them, but I ignored her and she didn't even notice them, so overwhelmed was she by the overall effect when she first saw it.

This job is one instance where the whole thing was organized almost entirely over the telephone as the client had already left the country and it wasn't physically possible for us to meet. This was nerve-wracking even for me and when I told her I was planning to use hessian – potato sacking – on the tables, she was so appalled that she sent a friend round to see what I was talking about. Fortunately we saw eye to eye, and the party was a tremendous success.

This photograph gives an overall view of the palace garden and shows how successful we were in combining the hostess' desire for a party that was both elegant and tropical. The velvety starlit sky was created by sewing small (Christmas tree style) lights onto a dark fabric, the result heightening the drama, excitement and sheer romance of the setting. The table in the foreground employs orchids and exotic fruits like grapes, melon and lemon in its oasis; around it is easy to imagine unfamiliar birds, rustling bamboo and the balmy warmth of the night.

143

A MEDITERRANEAN GARDEN

ABOVE This overview of the setting hints at the enormity of the task I was given, but at the same time shows the magnificent white façade that was at the heart of the inspiration of the scheme. The cavernous stage, quite distinct from the dining area supplied by the auditorium, is perfect for dancing. Note how each of the table decorations are individually conceived and executed yet conform to the overall theme.

RIGHT We placed the top table centrally both so that the bride and groom could look around them and see all their guests and so that their guests could see them. The two large decorations at either end of the table have been carefully designed in two tiers so that the view is not obscured by them. The small overflowing baskets of cherries and strawberries, a deliberate contrast with the muted colours of the larger pieces, are as mouthwatering as the overall setting is stimulating to the rest of the senses.

When a young bride asked me to meet her at the Brixton Academy to discuss the plans for her wedding reception I was flabbergasted. That area of London has a very poor reputation, moreover I had no idea what the Academy building looked like. In the event I was rather appalled when we did find it, as it turned out to be a former cinema now used as a venue for rock concerts. Inside the place was filthy and there was this huge open space, where the seats had been taken out, sloping down to the stage. But the stage itself was magnificent: the backdrop the facade of an Italian palazzo with a balustrade running round the edge. The obvious thing to do was to transform the whole of the auditorium into the garden of the palace on stage. The job was enormous, and a little daunting, but the challenge was very exciting. In the end it took three months of planning and three days to set up.

We had the whole of the interior painted and installed a false floor designed to look like a terrace. I wanted to extend the balustrade on the stage, so we had one made, crafted to look like sandstone. The guests were received in a room upstairs, where the decoration was art deco and flowers kept very simple. Then, when dinner was announced, they were piped into the auditorium: the doors were thrown open and they walked down steps into a paved garden and on into a gazebo complete with statues, that I had created on the stage for dancing.

To achieve the effect of a lush Mediterranean garden we brought in birch trees fifteen to twenty feet high, hundreds of climbing roses, thousands of gerbera, delphiniums and lilies, thousands of boxes of fruit – strawberries, raspberries and cherries. We used projectors and lighting to create special effects on the ceiling of the moon momentarily disappearing behind scudding clouds: the result was magnificent and the effect on the guests devastating. The wedding itself was very traditional and took place in a church in Knightsbridge. After the ceremony the guests were put into coaches and brought the few miles here, totally unprepared for the visual feast that awaited them. The element of surprise was emphasized because of the contrast of the surroundings – no-one could have expected that unprepossessing exterior to reveal such a glorious setting for a banquet – and it shows what it is possible to achieve with careful planning and a creative imagination.

The value of the well-grown birch trees is here shown where they help give a sense of proportion between the palace façade and its garden, where the guests are dining. The construction of terraces and the continuation of the balustrade allowed me to introduce a change of level, invaluable in creating variety particularly where the numbers to be seated are large. The balustraded walkways also provide a useful point of access to the dance floor from the auditorium.

RIGHT The gazebo which we created on the stage made a spectacular backdrop to the dancers. The white marble figures and dramatic explosion of colour supplied by the herbaceous flowers seemed to swirl with the motion of the music and provided a marked contrast with the more sober decorations among the diners.

AN EIGHTEENTH-CENTURY MASKED BALL

Venice is one of the most romantic cities in the world: the water, the gondolas and gondoliers, the decayed grandeur redolent of former glories, silent and beautiful churches, and all around the Italian sense of drama and fun. So when I was asked if I would create an eighteenth-century masked ball in a palazzo on the Grand Canal I leapt at the opportunity immediately. I plunged myself into the eighteenth century and considered the elaborate costumes of figures such as Marie Antoinette, the luxurious, extravagant life-styles, the lavish entertainment and the glorious style of everything they did. I wanted to make the ball as authentically eighteenth century as possible. I went to see the palace and was at once inspired by the architecture, by the pictures and by snatches of contemporary music. I began to build up a picture of what it could have been like to walk into a ballroom for a party in the eighteenth century and determined to transport the guests into that world. My client was thrilled by the ideas as I talked them through with him and I was given the go-ahead.

Many of the final details were inspired by pictures: the palette used by artists then was extraordinarily rich – burgundies, deep coral pinks and rich reds – and these were the colours that dominated my scheme. The dining-room was lit by the most brilliant chandeliers and it occurred to me how striking it would seem if they were linked with sweeping garlands and made to look as though they were suspended from the ceiling by ferns and not by chains. We continued the theme by bringing the garlands down to the candelabra on the table and then creating lesser decorations the whole length of it. There were two very long tables, crossed at the end by the high table and we decorated the chair backs one way for the ladies and another for the gentlemen all the way down. The effect was like a picture made from a delicate lattice-work of flowers and was so romantic and magical that you feared that if you looked away it would all disappear.

But the one hundred and fifty or so guests were taken back into the eighteenth century long before they came into dinner. They were brought in full costume by gondola right up to the steps of the palace, where fountains were playing into the water. They walked into a room inspired by *Phantom of the Opera*: there were fantastic topiaries, typical Venetian masks spouting smoke made from dry ice, and music playing gently in the background. The atmosphere was very mysterious and a little spooky. They were led on upstairs for drinks; around them the pillars were overgrown with vines of black grapes that appeared to be growing up through the floor, and from this they were brought into dinner where a carnival of flowers awaited them – a total contrast to the bizarre but austere effect that had preceded it.

LEFT Parties on such a grand scale as that in Venice take many months of planning and several days to set up. Here one of the blackamoors is having the final work done on his features to make sure they stand out. It is attention to details of this sort that makes a party an overwhelming success and distinguishes it from those where the same trouble has not been taken.

RIGHT The setting for this party meant had far less to do than normal in establishing the right ambience. The situation of the palace right on the Grand Canal could not have been bettered and the guests were brought by gondola to the steps of the palace and received into this entrance hall. Use of dry ice increased the already strong atmosphere of mystery and romance.

To see those costumed figures seated at the table, fêted by jesters and minstrels was, for me, a complete realization of my vision and an almost disturbing removal to another age.

But the surprises for the guests were not over, for during dinner the topiaries were removed and the entrance was transformed into a dance floor; an army of blackamoors supported fruit and flowers, and while the guests danced dry ice swirled and billowed, momentarily hiding their partner and then revealing them again like some fantastic dream.

The decoration of the dining room was perhaps the most exciting of the challenges that faced me in Venice. The indigenous decoration was already breathtaking and it was important that I in no way detracted from it: the room had a beautiful, painted ceiling, fine decorative plasterwork and marble panelling, wonderful, huge mirrors, elaborate wall sconces and the most exquisite chandeliers I have ever seen. It was in order not to diminish these, and in fact to draw attention to them, that I decided to hang garlands of fern between them and down to link them with the tall candelabra-cum-decorations on the tables. Between these smaller candlesticks ran the length of the table, themselves interspersed with short, slow-burning candles wrapped up in moss. The quality of light, enhanced by the shimmering reflections in the mirrors, was magical and the whole scene could have emerged straight from a fairytale. (See also photograph on pages 2–3.)

This exotic candelabra, one of the series lining the sides of the entrance hall when it transformed into a dance floor during dinner, is made from the statue of a blackamoor garlanded with a thick rope of exotic fruits – pineapples, grapes, bananas – gilded fern, lilies and roses. It conjures up images of Venice's heyday as a great maritime and trading power and as one of the richest, most exotic cities in the world.

No corridor and no ante-room could be left
undecorated in the transformation of this Venetian
palace. Here an extremely elegant inlaid writing
desk is playing host to a fittingly regal display
of fresh flowers. The soaring delphiniums, gladioli,
lilies and roses fill out the framework supplied by
the eucalyptus, hydrangea and trailing ivy, creating
a decoration of extraordinary vitality and vigour.

The whole occasion was like being permitted a glimpse of another world, like being taken back into another era, where romance coloured its inhabitants' view of life and sustained everything they did. In some ways the Venetian experience sums up everything I aspire to achieve on these occasions and with my decorations: to create a world that doesn't exist, to make-believe a universal atmosphere of romance and intrigue and to see people living within it.

The decoration of the chairs at the dinner table seemed appropriate in view of the grandeur and degree of attention to detail in the rest of the room. I thought it would be fun to decorate the chairbacks, in one style for the men and another for the women, so the pattern would alternate the whole length of the table. For the ladies I chose a bunch of soft pink roses, held together behind a traditional Venetian mask suggestive of the romance and intrigue that might be found behind it; for the gentlemen a bunch of red roses, finished with a masculine red and blue tassel, the hint of formality belied by the essential femininity of the rose.

CALENDAR OF IDEAS

January

arum leaves
catkins
dogwood
eucalyptus
forsythia/blossom brought into house
and forced out in the warmth
Garrya elliptica
hazel
Mahonia japonica (lily of the valley tree)
snowdrops
Viburnum fragrans
weeping willow
winter aconites
winter flowering cherry

February

Cornus mas (cornelian cherry)
dogwood
hellebore
irises
Japonica (quince)
pussy willow
reticulata
senecio greyii/davidii
winter sweet (*chimonanthus*)
witch hazel (*Hamamelis mollis*)

March

anemones
camellias
Cornus mas (cornelian cherry)
crocus
early botanical tulips
early rhododendrons
euphorbia
narcissi
hellebore
hyacinth
prunus
Viburnum tinus
witch hazel (*Hamamelis mollis*)

April

artichoke leaves
azaleas
balm poplar
blossom – prunus/pear/almond
cistus (*janista*)
clematis
cowslips
forsythia
hostas
Kerria japonica
magnolia
polyanthus
primroses
Ribes (flowering currant)
tulips

May

angelica
azaleas
bluebells
buttercups
dianthus
ceanothus
cow's parsley
dicentris
early red peonies
guelder rose
hostas
lily of the valley
rhododendrons
syringa (lilac)
Viburnum opulus sterile

June

Alchemilla mollis
all foliage
angelica
clematis
delphinium
dianthus
foxgloves
honeysuckle
larkspur
Lilium regale
lupins
oriental poppies
peonies
philadelphus
roses – climbing and shrub
spiraea
wild geranium
wild hemlock
wild rosebriar

July

acanthus
achillaea
allium
astilbe
deutzia
nicotiana
nigella
hogweed
hollyhocks
hydrangeas
jasmine
kniphofia
lavender
phlox
roses
salvia
scabious
sweet peas

August

acanthus
agapanthus
annuals – cornflowers, marigolds
amaranthus
buddleia
escallonia
geraniums
godetia
herbs – chives, lovage, marjoram, sage,
rosemary, fennel
hydrangeas
lilies (auretum)
nicotiana
pelargoniums
polygonum
roses
sedum
zinnias

September

antirrhinums
blackberries
cabbage – ornamental
cotoneaster
dahlias
delphiniums
euonymus
gladioli (for some!)
hips
Korean chrysanthemums (*never* use
blooms)
larkspur
Magnolia grandiflora
mushrooms/fungi
old man's beard
roses
seedheads – fennel, hogweed, allium
sloes
tomatoes

October

amaryllis
apples/pears/fruits
artichokes
asters
belladonna
elderberries
golden rod
gourds
hawthorn
Michaelmas daisies
hazelnuts
pumpkins
seedheads
Spanish chestnuts
tinted foliages
wheat/corns/grasses

November

This is a most difficult month and you
may need to resort to market flowers.
Dried flowers also come into their own
at this time of year.
camellia foliage
eleagnus
foliage – rhododendron, laurel
Magnolia grandiflora
moss
stones
wood

December

anything dried!
berried ivy
cinnamon sticks
cones
Christmas roses
eucalyptus
goltheria
gourds
hollies
ivies
juniper
larch
lichen
magnolia leaves
mistletoe
nutmeg
nuts
pines
pomegranates
winter cherry
winter jasmine

INDEX

ACKNOWLEDGEMENTS

My work and the success of my business, Kenneth Turner Flowers, has been largely due to the extraordinary kindness and help that has been given to me over the years by institutions, companies and individuals – many of whom have become valued friends. This friendship and support has enabled me to release the creative powers of my imagination and to realize my dreams.

My personal thanks go especially to

Lauren Bacall
The Duke of Beaufort
Mark Birley
Pilar Boxford
Godfrey and Susan Bradman
Di Camden
Robert Carrier
Jack and Anellia Cates
Neville and Carol Conrad
Fleur Cowles
Ronnie and Misty Driver
Moise and Rina Elghanayan
John and Susan Gutfreund
Gilda Gourlay
Rod and Jenny Hall
Pamela, Lady Harlech
George Harrison
Lynne Hazandrous
David Hicks
Geoffrey and Sally James
Joyce James
Tessa Kennedy
HRH The Princess Michael of Kent
HRH The Duchess of Kent
Nancy Lancaster
Gemma Levine

Jenny McAlpine
Sarah McAlpine
Dawn Mello
Paul and Bunny Mellon
Jack Menaged
David Milinaric
Ira Niemark
Mimi O'Connell
Jackie Onassis
Tom Parr
Claudine Pereira
Earl and Countess of Plymouth
Gail Ronson
Mortimer and Theresa Sackler
Lily Saffra
Mrs Salzburger
Maurice and Charles Saatchi
Julian Seymour
Belle Shenkman-Smith
Lady Spencer
Roy Strong
Lady Tryon
Bea Tollman
Drew Heinz
Lady Weinberg
Jayne Wrightsman

And to many more too numerous to mention

Above all I would like to thank my close and talented team, without whose wonderful and enthusiastic support much of the work in this book would never have been done.

The publishers and I would also like to thank all those who have helped make this book possible:

Asprey plc
Mrs Black
Mark Birley
Jack and Anneilia Cates
Chinacraft
Mrs Cohen
Christine Corson
Mrs D. Crutchley
Jacqueline Geddes
Thomas Goode
Harry Green
Rod and Jenny Hall
Sally James
Mrs Kovas

Lalique
Jenny McAlpine
Sarah McAlpine
John Miller
Sue Nicholls
Lady Nuttall
Mr Nabil Obayda
Andrew Phillips
Caroline Roboh
Theresa Sackler
Fritz von der Schulenburg
Keith Skeel Antiques
John Spikes

PHOTOGRAPHIC ACKNOWLEDGEMENTS

The photographs in this book were taken by the photographers as follows:

John Miller pages 1–6, 10, 17–18, 20–21, 24–29, 31, 36 (bottom), 39, 42, 44–7, 49, 55 (left), 56–9, 62–3, 65–7, 69–71, 73 (left), 74 (top), 78, 80–82, 84–5, 88–92, 94–105, 107, 109–10, 114–19, 132, 134–7, 147–9, 151–4, 158 © George Weidenfeld and Nicolson 1989

Fritz von der Schulenburg pages 13, 22, 30, 32–5, 36 (top), 37–8, 40, 43, 48, 52–4, 55 (right), 64, 72, 74 (bottom), 75–6, 93, 106, 111–13, 122–5, 126 (top), 127–30, 137, 140–46 © Fritz von der Schulenburg 1989

Clive Bournsell pages 8, 9, 14, 16, 51, 73 (right), 77, 83, 86, 87, 108, 126 © George Weidenfeld and Nicolson 1989

© David Montgomery 1989 page 121

page 120 kindly supplied by Thomas Goode

pages 19, 68, 121 (© David Montgomery 1989), 131 kindly supplied by Kenneth Turner Flowers

page 1 Giant hogweed, dried, at home in my sitting-room (see page 36).

pages 2–3 The dining-room in a Venetian palazzo, decorated for a masked ball (see pages 148–55).

pages 4–5 This rustic table, complete with up-turned terracotta pots, moss tablecloth and cushions, trails of ivy and rustic candelabra, the chairbacks decorated with cow's parsley and bamboo, brings to life Titania's feast in *A Midsummer Night's Dream*.

Title page Lilies, roses, Canterbury bells and euphorbia combine with ivy, artichoke and senecio foliage to devastating effect in this formal, more traditional decoration.

Imprint This small topiary-like sculpture has been made from eucalyptus and the base of the container lined with lichen.

Dedication The simplicity of this decoration, with the moss bursting out from the rough wicker basket, allows the lilies to be appreciated to the full.

Contents Dragon tulips, a gorgeous pink camellia, and delicate pink blossom attempt to attract the bust's attention, lit from a rustic candelabra.

Endpaper The 'trophy' design from my fabric range. These are distributed by Dovedale Fabrics Ltd, Caerphilly Road, Ystrad Mymach, Mid Glamorgan CF8 7EP.